THE
RICH *go to*
HEAVEN

THE RICH *go to* HEAVEN

GIVING CHARITY IN JEWISH THOUGHT

ELI M. SHEAR
CHAIM MILLER

JASON ARONSON INC.
Northvale, New Jersey
Jerusalem

This book was set in 12 pt. Antiqua by Alpha Graphics of Pittsfield, New Hampshire.

Library of Congress Cataloging-in-Publication Data
Shear, Eli M.
    The rich go to heaven : giving charity in Jewish thought / by Eli M. Shear and Chaim Miller.
        p.   cm.
    Includes bibliographical references and index.
    ISBN 0-7657-5990-X (alk. paper)
    1. Charity.   2. Ethics, Jewish.   3. Charity laws and legislation (Jewish law)   4. Judaism and social problems.   I. Miller, Chaim. II. Title.
BJ1286.C5S48   1997
296.3'677—dc21   97-7747

Manufactured in the United States of America. Jason Aronson Inc. offers books and cassettes. For information and catalog write to Jason Aronson Inc., 230 Livingston Street, Northvale, New Jersey 07647.

Dedicated to the Rebbe

"For his outstanding and lasting contributions
toward improvements in world education,
morality, and *acts of charity*."

—from Bill to bestow Congressional Gold Medal
on the Rebbe, 1994

With thanks to Hilary and Cyril Dennis
of London, England

For inspiring Anglo-Jewry with the profundity
and the beauty of their charitable gifts.

Contents

Acknowledgments

About five years ago, while undergraduate students at university in England, we stumbled, through a series of personal encounters, upon the vast collection of essays of the Lubavitcher Rebbe, Menachem Mendel Schneersohn. Despite the fact that the Rebbe's essays discussed topics of which we had little comprehension, involved multilayered analysis of ideas, and were almost exclusively in Yiddish, they immediately appealed directly to the mind and to the heart. Ingenious in originality and immense in scope, the Rebbe would take a subtle textual nuance in a Jewish work as the starting point for a long journey. He would first examine the ways in which classical solutions are unsatisfactory and unsatisfying, and then progress into deep expositions of purpose and reality which, when fully developed, would answer all of the earlier difficulties, leaving the reader with a sense of warmth and direction. More sophisticated than a mathematical equation, but with the appeal of sweet poetry, these essays revealed a different, distant world—but one that was somehow as familiar as home.

The following chapters are based on the Rebbe's essays on *tzedakah*, and thus anything of value within this volume is attributable to his wisdom. The intellectual inspiration to write this book came from the Rebbe, whilst personal guidance has also come from a number of others.

Thanks are extended for the original stimulus in our lives from the "Sufrins of Ilford." University inspiration came from Rabbis Yirmeyahu Angyalfi, Jonathan Dove, and Shmuel Boteach. At yeshivah, the primary spark was ignited by the scholarship, humor, and profound erudition of Rabbi Alter Metzger, and was continued by Rabbis Avromel Lipsker, Moshe Herson, Chaim Brofman, and Yosef Yitzchak Greenberg.

We were ultimately blessed to have been taught by two of the finest teachers and exemplar Chassidim of this generation: Rabbi Yosef-Yitzchak ("Fitzy") Lipsker z"l and Rabbi Dovid Wichnin z"l—who personified everything that is beautiful within this book.

The original manuscript of this work was read by Rabbi Nissan Mangel (in part) and Rabbis Tzvi Telsner and Michoel Chanoch Golomb. Editing was undertaken by Shlomo Lapon; computer assistance and much encouragement were given by Avraham Tzvi Burdman; and typing assistance was provided by Daniel Brooks, David Tivony, Tzvi Meir Kriegsman, Yitzchak Gazlan, and Yehoshua Rees.

Two "Zeidies" require specific mention. Jacob Newman, a master storyteller, provided most of the funniest jokes in this work; and Joseph Graham o.b.m. inspired a love for the mitzvah of *tzedakah* through a life overflowing with acts of philanthropy.

Finally, to the Shear and Miller families for their support and motivation; and particularly Leah Shear, for encouraging this work (and for being a wife who makes me constantly aware that God is infinitely charitable.—E.M.S.).

1

Coin of Fire

The two Jews stranded on the desert island could hardly have been more different in attitude. The first scurried desperately around the island, attempting by signals, noises, and any other means possible to attract the attention of a passing ship. The second Jew simply laid back, read a "good book," and basked in the glorious sunshine.

"I really don't understand it," gasped the first Jew, after exhausting himself for several hours. "We could be deserted on this island forever, and you're not doing anything at all to try to save us."

As he removed a large Cuban cigar from his mouth, the second Jew appeased his friend: "Look, there's really no cause for alarm. I donated a million dollars to the Jewish Israel Fund last year, and they have another appeal next week. Don't worry, they'll find me!"

Despite any stereotypes of frugality, the simple fact is that Jews give lots of money to charity. This is not only statistically provable[1] or manifest in the disproportionate number of cases in English charitable law which concern Jews as donors, but also in the well-known history of Jewish philanthropy.

From Abraham to the Rothschilds, the mitzvah of *tzedakah* has always been well-observed. In her recent autobiography, Margaret Thatcher, the British prime minister from 1979 until 1991, expressed "enormous admiration" for the Jewish approach to charity, and stated that in her 33 years as a politician, "I never had a Jew come in poverty or desperation to one of my constituency surgeries. They had always been looked after by their own community."[2]

While charity is recognized as a moral act by all societies, for the Jew it has an added dimension. *Tzedakah* is an obligation imposed upon every individual: "Giving charity to the poor according to one's means" is among the 613 mitzvahs (commandments),[3] and is therefore not a matter of choice, but of duty. However, any suggestion that to enforce the duty spoils the act, that it replaces selflessness and altruism with fear of Divine reprisal, fails to appreciate exactly what a mitzvah is.

The principal mistake is in the word mitzvah itself, which best translates as "connection" (the etymological root being *tzavsa*).[4] When a Jew performs the mitzvah of *tzedakah*, he is not merely satisfying his moral conscience, but with the very act of giving he is connecting with his Creator. This makes the Jew's ac-

---

1. Stephen D. Issacs, *Jews and American Politics* (Garden City, NY: Doubleday, 1974).

2. Margaret Thatcher, *The Downing Street Years* (HarperCollins, 1993), p. 509.

3. Deut. 15:11.

4. *Igres Kodesh* of the Rebbe, vol 6 (Kehot Publication Society [KPS], 1988), pp. 1–2.

tion unlimited in scope and achievement.[5] He is *connecting* with the infinite. His act is not merely good or spiritual, but Godly.

BIG BUSINESS ON THE SMALL MOUNTAIN

When the 613 mitzvahs were given at Mount Sinai and the voice of God was heard by more than two million witnesses, the Midrash explains that as God spoke, "no echo was heard."[6] While this appears a somewhat strange and unnecessary comment, it actually captures the essence of Sinai, and the innovation of a mitzvah. An echo is explained in physics as similar to a bouncing ball—the reflection of a sound off a surface. The fact that no echo was heard at Sinai expresses the miraculous occurrence that all physical surfaces from which God's words should have been reflected actually ab-

---

5. In the history of human civilization, the ideas and theories of any individual, however great his genius, are limited by an inability to appreciate the effect such an idea will have over time. Not so with the Jew. For more than 3,000 years, there has always been a group of Jews performing mitzvahs with the absolute conviction that each act has a significance that will never fade away. The limitation of all history's great thinkers is in their inability to visualize the practical consequences of their theories. Karl Marx may never have written *Das Kapital* if he could have predicted that it would be the blueprint for a totalitarian bureaucracy that justified the torture and butchery of millions of its citizens. Charles Darwin was a firm believer in God, and may not have written *The Origin of Species* had he known it would become the bible of atheism for the scientifically ignorant.

6. *Shemos Rabbah*, end of ch. 28.

sorbed His voice.[7] All physical objects became per-
meated with the voice of God, and this elevated the
mundane and physical to the very heights of spirituality and holiness. While other religions advocate regular fasting, meditation, and celibacy, the Jew after Sinai
is positively encouraged to involve himself in things
physical and thereby reveal the Godly sparks that were
hidden at the time of creation and that are now capable
of being revealed.

Judaism emphasizes deed rather than creed;[8] and
each deed necessitates the use of physical objects.
Thinking about the spirituality of tefillin is not the
mitzvah, wearing them is. Pitying the poor is not the
mitzvah of *tzedakah*, giving them money is. Sinai ensured that the means to spirituality would be by physical deeds, and so the act of giving charity was no longer
limited to the corporeal parameters of human understanding. The advantage of connecting to the infinite
and accessing the ethereal through physical matter
became the extra dimension that distinguishes the
mitzvah of *tzedakah* from the moral act of charity.

A NEW DIMENSION TO CONNECTING

In the Babylonian Talmud there is a remarkable dialogue between God and Moses.[9] This occurs only a
short period after the Revelation at Sinai, where the
Jews had been elevated from their status as slaves in
Egypt to that of "a nation of princes and holy people."[10]

---

7. *Likutei Sichos*, 6th ed., vol. 4 (KPS, 1992), pp. 1092–
1098.
8. *Pirkei Avos* 1:7.
9. *Bava Basra* 10b.
10. Exod. 19:6.

At a time when most leaders would be more than satisfied with such a change in standing, Moses pleaded to God, "by what means can the strength of the Jewish people be increased?"

This question of Moses is staggering when one considers that Sinai was an occasion when every Jew clearly heard the voice of God,[11] and was raised to the level of a prophet. Would not the appropriate response to such a quantum leap in status be inexhaustible gratitude rather than an additional request for power that expresses all of the *chutzpah* of "Please, sir, I want some more."

Such a question coming from any person other than Moses might well seem suspicious. However, the fact that it was asked by an individual whose decision making and self-effacement have been admired throughout history leaves no room to question the appropriateness of this particular request. It is axiomatic that Moses does not ask rude or unnecessary questions. His words have been carefully dissected by generations of Torah scholars, and to cherish his every utterance is a fundamental principle of the Jewish religion.[12] If Moses wanted more for his people than Sinai had provided, one can be certain that God still had more to offer.

In response to Moses's vision of a Judaism that would reach beyond Sinai, God's answer was the seemingly mundane plan of establishing a new charity fund. The Talmud states that God's response was the specific request that every Jew contribute a half-shekel towards the construction of the Tabernacle. It therefore appears that God had designed a unique role for the giving of

---

11. Exod. 20:15.

12. Rambam, *Commentary to the Mishnah, Sanhedrin,* "perek Chelek."

tzedakah in His creation; yet how could He imply that
the establishment of a simple communal fund could
exceed the achievement of Sinai, which joined the
physical world with its spiritual source?

Nevertheless, the most remarkable aspect of God's
response is how the Divine intellect could propose a
plan which appears so lacking in originality. Charity
existed as a moral value long before the Jews existed
as a people.[13] Not only has the human conscience always been predisposed to acts of kindness, but it has
been a moral obligation respected throughout the history of the civilized world. The Bible[14] records that the
inhabitants of Sodom were punished with the destruction of their entire city due to a failure to help the
poor.[15] Finally, charity was elevated at Sinai to the level
of a mitzvah, making any gift to *tzedakah* an act of
unprecedented significance. Consequently, since all
mitzvahs are infinite, and so must be considered equal,
what is so special about the mitzvah of *tzedakah*, that
it could increase "Jewish strength" more than any of
the other mitzvahs?

FINDING SANCTUARY BELOW

An answer is provided by the Maharsha (Rabbi Shmuel
Eliezer Eidels, 1555–1632), one of the foremost Talmu-

---

13. Gen. 18:19.

14. Ezek. 16:49; see also chapter 7, below.

15. Benevolence is, in fact, so instinctual that it is not
only a human emotion but extends across the Animal Kingdom. Honeybees and ants are renowned for their intricate
"social" structures in which individual organisms take
upon themselves burdensome tasks on behalf of the entire
community.

dic commentators, whose insights were so profound that the Baal Shem-Tov praised him by saying, "If the world knew his true holiness, they would lick the earth that is on his grave." He explains that the new charity fund, consisting of individual gifts of one half-shekel, was not a mere donation to charity, but rather a direct contribution to the holy Tabernacle, an edifice within which the *Shechina* (Divine Presence) chose to dwell.[16] On this basis, the Maharsha concludes that since the half-shekel led to the manifestation of the *Shechina* in the Jewish camp, Moses's request for the elevation of his people would be achieved—since God's presence in one's camp brings with it ultimate strength. The half-shekel may have appeared mundane after Sinai, but it was actually the key to an unimaginable privilege: God would now be the "roommate" of the Jews.[17]

It was exactly this privilege which the wise men of Chelm sought to acquire, with their famous plan to construct a perfect replica of the Tabernacle in their synagogue grounds. A formal meeting was convened, at which the Board of Management of the Chelm synagogue was to vote on whether to award the plan permission and give their approval for this bold innovation. After the president of the Board announced that the construction of their own personal Tabernacle would ensure that the Divine presence would dwell in Chelm, the vote was called. The president was, however, totally unable to control his surprise and disgust when the expected unanimous verdict was spoiled by one lone dissenter: the synagogue's old and learned rabbi.

"While I commend your enthusiasm," exclaimed the wise rabbi, "you must realise that to build a Taber-

---

16. *Chiddushei Aggados Maharsha, Bava Basra* 10b.
17. Midrash *Tanchuma, Tisa* 5.

nacle here in Chelm is totally prohibited according to Jewish law."

The president was unmoved, and proceeded to argue that the publicity and honor of having the *Shechina* dwell in Chelm far outweighed any legal difficulties. "The vote is ten against one, and so the Tabernacle will be built," the president insisted. The rabbi pleaded tirelessly against the plan, and eventually, close to tears, he challenged that if he was right, a voice from heaven would speak out in his support.

"YOUR RABBI IS CORRECT," boomed a heavenly voice, "THE PLANNED CHELM TABERNACLE IS AN ABOMINATION. YOU WILL ALL BE PUNISHED FOR THIS IDOLATROUS ACT."

"Alright, I give in," shrieked the president from his hiding place under the table, "ten votes against two!"

To construct an unauthorized Tabernacle may very well be an act of idol-worship in Jewish law, yet it could be argued such a desire is based upon a valid Jewish emotion: The need to connect with God in a tangible manner.[18] The inhabitants of Chelm may be somewhat stupid, but they are also very Jewish. Whilst their approach may be dubious, their ultimate goal is admirable: to welcome God down from the heavens into their synagogue.

If it was the half-shekel that caused the *Shechina* to dwell on earth (by means of the Tabernacle), then this single coin was surely the key to immense power. The Maharsha makes sense of the dialogue between God and Moses by explaining the goal of the half-shekel to be the dwelling of the *Shechina* in the Taber-

---

18. The mistake is that the means of connection must be at the discretion of the superior being. See *Likutei Sichos*, vol. 24 (KPS, 1984), pp. 1–11.

nacle. It was the pursuit of such a goal that Moses envisioned as the means to increasing the strength of the Jewish people beyond the innovation of Sinai.

COIN OF FIRE

However, in a deeper sense, the Maharsha does not present us with a solution, but rather makes the question even larger. Even if it were now understood exactly *how* charity was to be the vehicle by which the Jews would progress beyond Sinai, it must first be understood *why* it was charity that God singled out as the means by which He would dwell among the Jews? He could have chosen anything—a secret password, a ritual dance, chopping wood—and the *Shechina* would come down. From God's perspective, the ends are not determined by the means: any result, such as bringing down the *Shechina*, can be achieved by any method. Therefore, there must be a distinctive quality of *tzedakah* that merited it to be the chosen means for bringing Godliness down into the Jewish camp.[19]

Rashi (Rabbenu Shlomo ben Yitzchak Yarchi of medieval France, 1040–1105), author of the most important commentaries on the Torah and Talmud, explains the significance of the biblical command to give half a shekel by stating, "God showed him (Moses) a *Coin of Fire*, whose weight was half a shekel, and told him 'they should give a coin like this.'"[20]

---

19. Piyut "*Lecha Dodi*," "Last in Creation, first in [God's] thought," *Siddur Tehillas Hashem*, p. 32. KHP—1987.

20. Rashi on Exod. 30:13, from *Shekalim* 1:5 and Midrash *Tanchuma*, *Tisa* 9.

This midrashic tale appears somewhat strange, since fire has no shape or form,[21] as it is fluctuating continuously, while the reverse is true of a coin (for its very value depends upon its shape.[22]) Furthermore, a coin is pulled downward by gravity, whereas fire ascends naturally, and with such force that a wick is required to restrain it. Therefore, a *Coin of Fire* is a contradiction in terms: a fusion of two things which are absolute opposites.[23]

PHILOSOPHY OF FIRE

The constant ascent of fire is a form of escapism. Its true desire is to leave its present existence and return to its source above.[24] Consequently, fire is formless, since it does not remain in the same state, and constantly attempts to change its shape.

It could therefore be argued that fire represents the infinite, which cannot be confined to any form or limitation. Conversely, the vision of a Coin of Fire signifies the infinite quality of fire, bound together with the finite form and weight of a coin. A spiritual oxymoron—and precisely the quality that *tzedakah* boasts.

The act of *tzedakah* has many possible motivations, such as a good nature,[25] or the knowledge that one is fulfilling a societal duty. A much higher level than giving for intellectual or emotional reasons is

---

21. Rambam, *Hilchos Yesodei Hatorah*, beginning of ch. 4.
22. *Bava Metzia* 45b; Rashi, *"Mshum D'daiti."*
23. *Likutei Sichos*, vol. 26 (KPS, 1988), p. 233.
24. *Tanya (Likutei Amarim)*, ch 19.
25. *Yevamos* 79a.

based on the fact that God commanded that one must give *tzedakah*. Nevertheless, even this level of charity could be "limited," possibly by the desire for personal reward.[26]

An even higher level of giving is a person who fulfils the mitzvah without the intention of receiving a reward. Yet it may be that this itself is his intention; the person wants to perform the mitzvah as it is his nature to be "religious."[27] Even though this is incomparably higher than doing a mitzvah for personal gain, it is nonetheless connected to a motive, a desire to do God's will (religiosity). Consequently, the fulfillment of the mitzvah is connected with a form and limitation, as it is confined by the motivation which led to it.

"TO DO THE TRUTH, BECAUSE IT IS TRUE"

The ultimate level in the observance of a Jew[28] according to the Rambam (Rabbi Moshe ben Maimon 1135–1204),[29] is to observe "not because of worldly matters, and not because of fear of evil, and not in order to inherit good," and even "not to merit life in the world to come," because this is still connected with his nature

---

26. An example of this is a person who fulfils the mitzvah of *tzedakah* in order to earn a promised reward, either physical (the Talmud in Tractate *Pesachim* 8a states that the reward for giving *tzedakah* is life for your children, etc.) or spiritual (Tractate *Peah* 1:1 promises a reward in the world to come, etc.).

27. See *Sefer Hasichos* 5704/1944 (KPS, 1973), p. 5.

28. In truth, the expression "ultimate" is inappropriate because it is a definition and thus has the limitation of being "mere perfection."

29. Rambam, *Hilchos Teshuvah*, ch. 10.

and consequently connected to a form. Rather, observance should be, as Maimonides concludes, "To do the truth because it is true"—not because of any ulterior motive.

It is this highest level of giving *tzedakah*, which was depicted to Moses by the image of the Coin of Fire. Moses was troubled by the question, "By what means can the strength of the Jewish people be increased?" as it appeared that to be a mitzvah was the greatest privilege that any act could attain. Nevertheless, mitzvahs were still actions which took place in the world, and every human activity within the world is limited by the fact that it must have a motive. An act can only be as effective as the person who performs it.[30]

Therefore, even though a mitzvah is a Godly act, which transcends mere physicality, the very fact that it is performed by a human being limits its scope. Moses wanted the Jews to have mitzvahs that could be totally altruistic, escaping all the confines of the world, since only a totally infinite activity can form a perfect connection to the infinite God. Moses understood that even if *tzedakah* was given for the most lofty, religious, and spiritual of reasons, those reasons would be themselves limitations.

God responded to this request with the image of a Coin of Fire, which contained three significant components: (i) The fire, which represents total altruism. Fire does not wish to "be for itself," but constantly yearns upward to escape its own existence. (ii) The

---

30. See *Avos* 1:3 and *Tanya*, ch. 40, where mitzvahs are compared to a bird, the wings being love and fear of God. Hence, if the "intention" is missing, the mitzvah still exists—like a bird without wings, it is incapable of flying, which is its very purpose.

coin, which represents shape, form, and weight, all the characteristics of the world. However, the most important aspect of the image of the fiery coin is: (iii) The fact that the coin and the fire were one and the same. This provided the key answer for Moses, that it is possible for an act within the world to be totally altruistic, just as a coin can consist totally of fire.[31]

A Coin of Fire is a paradox: a contradiction in terms, like a motiveless act by a human being. However lofty the inspiration for a person to perform an act of kindness, or a mitzvah, it can still be limited to some form of motivation, even if it is noble and religious. In fact, if a person does an act of kindness merely for the sake of altruism, that itself is a limitation. Nevertheless, God showed Moses a Coin of Fire, which signified that, contrary to the laws of nature, and even the laws of religion, it was now possible to perform a physical mitzvah without being limited by any motivation; thereby, an increase in the strength of the Jewish people could be achieved. This was specifically through the mitzvah of *tzedakah*, because *tzedakah* means righteousness not simply for the sake of being righteous, but pure righteousness.

This level of righteousness is illustrated by the level of "To do the truth, because it is true"—not because of any reason (or even because of the reason that there is no reason); rather, the mitzvah is done through an essential connection with God. This connection of essence cannot be deemed a "reason" or motivation for observance because it is automatic, without any contemplation or inclination.

When Moses asked God, "By what means can the strength of the Jewish People be increased?" he was

---

31. *Sefer Hisvadiyus*, 5749/(KPS, 1989), p. 350.

asking the impossible: that a human should be able to perform an act of kindness without it being tarnished by human nature. God replied that the act of *tzedakah* is capable of this, since the very essence of *tzedakah* is righteousness—in the purest sense of the word.

2

Without Limits

The Jewish businessman travelled home with only one thing on his mind: Debt. His business was collapsing and there seemed no way to repay all his creditors, much less to support his family.

However, his eyes began to light up when he spotted a Church proudly offering a ten-thousand-dollar reward for any "on-the-spot conversion." Despite a great deal of unease, it was barely twenty minutes before the businessman emerged from the Church, the procedure completed, with a fistfull of dollars in his hand.

A few days later, the businessman's conscience was still troubling him, and so he decided to make an announcement in his local synagogue that all those requiring charity should appeal to him. That evening, caller after caller arrived at his doorstep, each one with a valid and moving plea; and the businessman proved unable to restrain himself. Having given away most of his money, he vowed to keep the remainder for himself.

At that very moment, a woman—with twelve children—arrived at the door and proceeded to tell a

heartrending story, climaxing in an urgent request for
a large sum of money. As the businessman peered into
his case, he saw that the amount she had asked for was
precisely the total remainder of his fortune.

As he handed over his last dollar to the woman,
the businessman cried out to the heavens, "Why is it
that as soon as we Gentiles get our hands on some
money, the Jews succeed in taking it away from us?"

SHOULD A PERSON EVER STOP GIVING CHARITY?

Anglo-American Law offers no direct guidelines in the
matter of an upper limit to charitable donations, and
considers the size of any gift to be at the absolute discretion of the giver. In a democracy, any limit on the
expenditure of an individual (so long as it is within his
means) would be considered an infringement upon his
rights; and the maximum level of any donation should
only be dictated by the generosity of the one who gives.

It may therefore come as something of a surprise
that Jewish law clearly prescribes an upper limit for
charitable donations. The Rambam (one of the greatest codifiers of law in Jewish history) writes in his
Mishneh Torah (a comprehensive statement of the laws
of a Torah society), "Even though charitable donations
[to the Temple] are a mitzvah . . . a man should never
give all his money for this purpose. . . . This would not
be piety but folly since he deprives himself and will
be driven to rely on others. One should not distribute
more than one-fifth."[1]

---

1. *Mishneh Torah, Hilchos Aruchin V'Charamin, Laws of
Valuations and Dedications*, 8:12–13.

The words of the Rambam in the *Mishneh Torah* are not advice, but law.[2] It thus appears that one is prohibited from donating any more than twenty percent of one's wealth to charity.[3] Therefore, those who are so unreservedly benevolent in their gifts to charity, exceeding the limit of one-fifth, actually appear to be committing a sin.

UNLIMITED GENEROSITY

Equity and a higher limit are, however, advocated in the writings of R. Shneur Zalman of Liadi (1745–1813), affectionately known as the Alter Rebbe. In the fifth book of his magnum opus, the *Tanya*, he states, "A Jew can give all his money away, and make donations without limit, as it rectifies the stumbling and blemish of his sins."[4]

Thus, the freedom to give as much as one desires does not only appear to have been restored, but a new obligation to give considerably more seems to have been established. The Alter Rebbe writes that "Everyone who fears the word of God is now accustomed to give vast amounts to *tzedakah* . . . without limits."[5]

How is it acceptable that the Alter Rebbe can hold that *tzedakah* should be given "without limits" when the Rambam clearly rules that "one should not distribute more than one-fifth"?

---

2. The Talmud explicitly states, "One who gives to charity should not give more than one-fifth in case he himself will need the support of others" (Tractate *Kesubos* 50a).

3. *Iggeres Hakodesh*, ch. 10.

4. Based on Job 2:4.

5. *Iggeres Hateshuvah*, ch. 3.

IRRECONCILABLE DIFFERENCES?

Although this appears to be a giant clash of Torah personalities, the view of the Rambam himself does not appear to be consistent. In his *Perush Hamishnayos* (*A Commentary on the Mishnah*), the Rambam explains, "there is a limit, which is one-fifth of one's wealth, and one is not obliged to give more than one-fifth of one's wealth, unless he [chooses to] do so through piety."[6] How could the Rambam present and encourage this option of giving large sums, and yet in his *Mishneh Torah* condemn such generous benefactors as displaying "folly" and explicitly forbid seemingly similar acts of altruism?[7]

---

6. *Commentary on the Mishnah, Peah* 1.

7. Whenever a difficulty with the Rambam arises for which there appears to be no straightforward answer, it is necessary to look into the sources which the Rambam himself used in order to reach his conclusions. The Rambam may be a great legal codifier, but in Jewish legal history he is a relatively recent arbitrator, and his decisions must be based upon the Talmud, which records the debates of the academies of ancient Babylon. In Tractate *Aruchin* of the Talmud (which discusses charitable donations to the Temple), there is an argument recorded between two *Tannaim* (highest legal authorities), who were discussing the issue of very large donations. Rabbi Eliezer is of the opinion that a person can donate his property in any amount he wishes, although he should not go so far as to offer everything he has, for any such donation would be invalid. Rabbi Eliezer Ben Azariah states that since God had mercy on a person and did not require him to give away all his property, all the more so should he himself have mercy on his own property.

The Gemmorah analyzes this discussion, concluding that these *Tannaim* are actually debating whether there should be an upper limit of one-fifth to charitable donation.

TWO MANNERS OF GIVING

All the difficulties concerning the upper limit for *tzedakah* can be resolved by appreciating that Jewish

---

The Gemorrah proves that R. Eliezer argues a person is allowed to give more than one-fifth of his property to charity. However, the "mercy" which R. Eliezer Ben Azariah requires an individual to have for his own possessions is, in practical terms, an upper limit of one-fifth.

With these sources clarified, there now appears an additional difficulty with the Rambam's ruling in his *Commentary on the Mishnah*. There he stated, "There is a limit, which is one-fifth of one's wealth, and one is not obliged to give more than one-fifth of one's wealth, unless he [chooses to] do so through piety." The Rambam does not have the authority to formulate a totally new opinion which has no precedent amongst the Tannaim, since they were responsible for transmitting the Oral Law as it was handed to Moses at Sinai. It is, however, the Rambam's prerogative to select an opinion from amongst the Tannaim, which he deems the most appropriate to be the final ruling, in the light of his vast knowledge.

However, since the Rambam decides that one-fifth is a sensible upper limit, but to give more is a "pious" thing to do, he has no source in the Talmud. He conflicts with Eliezer Ben Azariah's opinion that one-fifth is the limit, and any more is "not pious." On the other hand, he does not concur with R. Eliezer's opinion, which may consider large donations to be "pious," but makes no mention at all of the one-fifth figure.

Therefore, the Rambam not only seems to make two contradictory statements on this matter—in the *Mishnah Torah* (*Laws of Aruchin*) he fixes an upper limit of one-fifth, whereas in his *Commentary on the Mishnah* he praises those who break this rule as "pious"—but, a second problem is that his *Commentary on the Mishnah* seems to have no source in Jewish Law.

Law mandates several different levels of giving to charity. These classes of gift are defined according to the circumstances in which the donor and recipient find themselves.

The old Rabbi visited a mansion five times in one week, but on each occasion his continual ringing of the bell was met with no response. His enthusiasm undiminished, he made a note in his diary to return the next evening. However, as he was about to depart, the huge mansion gates opened electronically, and the master of the house returned in his chauffeur-driven Bentley.

"Excuse me, Sir. I don't mean to trouble you," exclaimed the old Rabbi, "but we have many large projects which we wish to undertake at our local synagogue. I wonder if you would be able to make a contribution?"

"Listen Rabbi, I'd really love to give," responded the millionaire as he walked towards his mansion. "The problem is I have a mother, very sick, in an old-age home which costs an absolute fortune. I have a wife in debt to six different credit-card companies, a son who needs to pay off the Mafia in order to avoid losing his life, and a daughter whose husband left her alone with nine children. I'm genuinely sorry, Rabbi," he said apologetically, "but if I don't give any of them a penny, I'm certainly not giving you. . . ."

There is a major difference between giving charity to a person who one understands to be in great need and random donations to "good causes." The millionaire's justification for not giving the old Rabbi any money is that there is a much "higher" level of charity, involving much more deserving recipients, which he chooses to neglect—how much more, then, will he not give the Rabbi's "less deserving" cause!

The Torah itself defines two such levels. There is a situation where a person wishes to give to charity and, while he is not aware of any particular individual who is in dire need, he knows that there are "worthy causes" and so decides to give to them. A totally different scenario is when a person is approached with a desperate plea by the recipient himself, and the donor can see in front of his eyes exactly what will be the consequences of his decision to give or not to give.

In the *Mishneh Torah*, the Rambam is discussing the "Laws of *Aruchin*," which concern voluntary contributions to the Temple, "a worthy cause." It is specifically in this type of giving that the Rambam rules that one-fifth is the upper limit and any more is "folly." However, in his *Perush Hamishnayos*, the situation is entirely different. Here the issue is "that a person sees captives who need to be redeemed, etc., or starving people or people without clothes." In such a situation, the Law differs, as an upper limit is deemed unreasonable. Consequently, the Rambam rules that a person is not obliged to give more than one-fifth, but to do so is "pious."[8]

TO GET OR TO GIVE

One possible reason for these two different types of *tzedakah* revolves around the question of who this

---

8. With this difference in situation clarified between the two sources, it is now understood why in his *Commentary on the Mishnah*, the Rambam does not follow any of the opinions in Tractate *Aruchin*. This Tractate deals with donations in the manner of "a worthy cause," and so any opinions mentioned here are unrelated to charity given in response to a desperate plea.

mitzvah is for—the donor or beneficiary? In the case
of giving to a worthy cause, such as the Temple, the
clear emphasis is on the donor, as he is giving in order
to be a righteous person.[9] Therefore, it would be fool-
ish for him to give so much that he suffered from the
donation. The law states that he should not give more
than one-fifth and to do so is "folly," because in order
to gain piety, he pays an unreasonable price.

In the case of a desperate plea, which corresponds
to a higher level of *tzedakah*, the giving is directed toward the needs of the beneficiary.[10] Here, it would be
unreasonable to limit the compassion of the giver, but
it would also be unreasonable to demand of him that
he give all his belongings. Hence, the Rambam rules
on this case in his *Perush Hamishnayos* that one-fifth
of his wealth is the maximum obligation, but to give
more is considered "pious."

THE THIRD LEVEL

However, a close examination of the Alter Rebbe's
words reveals two aspects which encourage the giving
of *tzedakah*, even more than the most generous view
of the Rambam: First, the Alter Rebbe denounces any
notion of the limit of one-fifth, whereas the Rambam
pays it some respect by claiming that it is the bound-
ary between the reasonable and the exceptional. Secondly, the Alter Rebbe actually advises that an individual should give "all" of his wealth to charity. The

9. *Shulchan Aruch HaRav, Orach Chayim* 156:3.
10. In his *Laws of the Poor*, ch. 7, the Rambam concurs
with this view, and states that the positive mitzvah is to
"give to the poor according to their needs," which provides
for a case exceeding one-fifth.

Rambam does not appear to agree with this opinion, since if he had thought it was permissible to give "all of one's wealth," he would not have stated the impressiveness of "more than one-fifth," but would have advised that a person should "give everything."[11]

Rather than to claim that the Alter Rebbe is arguing with the Rambam, it would make more sense to assume that he agrees with both of the Rambam's rulings, but the advice to give everything to charity is referring to an entirely different situation which is not discussed at all by the Rambam. In fact, the Alter Rebbe himself testifies to this, since he states that giving away all one's wealth is neither an expression of the righteousness of the donor, nor required by the needs of the recipient, but rather a type of "soul remedy."

Since *tzedakah* is deemed a modern substitute for penitential fasting (see chapter 4, below), the Alter Rebbe advises that "[t]he legal limit of one-fifth applies only to one who is free of sin or has already paid or fasted for his sins." One's health obviously take precedence over one's wealth, therefore, "[e]verything a person has, he can give to rescue his soul."

The Alter Rebbe lived several centuries after the Rambam, and considered his generation to be much more "spiritually sick" than those which had preceded. Thus his advice to give enormous amounts to *tzedakah* falls more under the category of "emergency medical treatment" for the soul than mere generosity or support of the poor. He explains that large amounts of charity should be given, since sins are now more prevalent, and the caliber of society is decidedly lower.

While remaining technically the mitzvah of *tzedakah*, the Alter Rebbe's charity has created an entirely

---

11. *Tzafonos Paneach* of the Rogatchover Gaon, on *Hilchos Aruchin*.

new application for giving money to the needy, which is not oriented toward benefiting the character of the giver, or supporting the beneficiary. It is considered more of a "life saving operation" to protect the integrity of the soul.[12]

EATING ON YOM KIPPUR

One year a plague struck the town of Brisk, and since many people were weak there was some fear that the fast of Yom Kippur would be a particularly difficult one. This was, however, a minor disturbance compared to the utter shock which passed throughout the community when the Brisker Rav himself (R. Chaim Soloveitchick, 1853–1918, who was famous for being very stringent in all of his legal rulings) instructed that fasting should not take place that year and everybody should eat as usual.[13] Finding such a great leniency somewhat difficult to accept, some of the foremost rabbis in his community approached the Rav, suggesting that perhaps there was no need to be so lenient in the laws of Yom Kippur, considering the seriousness of the day. "It's not that I am lenient with Yom Kip-

---

12. Implied in *Shulchan Aruch Harav*: "A person should give vast amounts with the qualities of abundance and kindness."

13. The Brisker Rav's followers were also punctilious in their observance, often going to extremes in the performance of mitzvot. For example, on the day preceding Yom Kippur, when it is a mitzvah to eat, they would be careful to suck boiled sweets throughout the entire day, so that there would not be one second when they would not be doing this mitzvah.

pur," explained the Rav, "but rather I'm stringent when there is a risk to life."

In a similar vein, the Alter Rebbe has advised that a Jew should give all of his money to charity, not because he is lenient with the rule of an upper limit, but because he is stringent with the spiritual welfare of the Jewish people.

A THIRD-LEVEL SERVANT

The three measures of giving *tzedakah*—one-fifth; more than one-fifth, but not all that one has; or the totality of one's wealth—correspond to three types of connection that an individual may experience with God.[14]

The first level corresponds to the person who serves God on an intellectual basis and performs mitzvahs because he is fully aware that they are the best possible actions he can perform, ensuring purpose and reward. Such a person is limited by his own intellect in the way he can connect with God. This level is represented by giving charity to a "worthy cause," where one's intentions are focused primarily on oneself, rather than upon holiness, and consequently the mitzvah is limited in both quality and quantity: one can give no more than one-fifth.

The second level of giving is directed toward fulfilling the needs of the beneficiary. Here, the donor is not so interested in exactly what the mitzvah will do for him as he is that God's will should be carried out, at whatever cost. This type of service is unlimited, and the Rambam rules that it is perfectly permissible to

---

14. *Iggeres Kodesh*, ch. 13.

give "more than one-fifth"—just as the motive does not have a limit, so too the sum which is given.

Nevertheless, such a service is not the highest manner in which a Jew can serve God, as there are still some factors at the discretion of the giver. Naturally, he will give as much as the beneficiary needs, but it remains a fact that he, himself, determines exactly how great these needs actually are. Therefore, since the Jew's sense of judgment plays some role in the mitzvah, it becomes tinged with a limitation, which renders it incapable of achieving a perfect connection with God.

The extent to which the judgment of the giver can distort the mitzvah of *tzedakah* is emphasized by the tale of the two brothers who would go begging every year at the house of a millionaire who would gladly send them away with $1000 each. However, one year only one beggar rang the bell of the mansion, still in mourning after his brother's recent passing.

"I'm terribly sorry to hear the news, and I hope this will help ease your pain," said the millionaire, as he handed over a large pile of money.

Ten minutes later, the beggar returned with the complaint, "There is only $1000 here, and you normally give $2000." The donor was startled, and after regaining his composure explained that the sad death of the beggar's brother made it impossible to give the second donation this year.

The beggar, totally unsatisfied with this answer, retorted, "So, since when did you become his principal beneficiary?"

While charity performed solely for the benefit of the recipient may be totally altruistic and selfless, connecting the donor with God in a manner which transcends human limitations, nevertheless, one limitation remains: the giver's discretion.

The distinctive quality of the third level is that, in the service of the Jew, there is no calculation or measurement whatsoever. This is a giving to *tzedakah* for the reason of a "risk to life," therefore every other consideration is ignored completely. Hence, all the Jew knows is that he wants to serve God, and he is willing to go to any extreme to restore his soul to its original perfect state—by whatever means necessary, even if it is totally unreasonable, extremely expensive, or seemingly impossible. If giving away all his money to *tzedakah* is the only way he can connect to God, he will do it. The individual feels that nothing in his life matters besides the fact that he is a Jew who must serve God. Correspondingly, the Alter Rebbe permits and even recommends that a person should give "all" of his wealth to charity.

From a deeper perspective, it can be appreciated that the entire suggestion of an upper limit to *tzedakah* signifies limitations within the performance of mitzvah themselves.[15] In his ruling, the Alter Rebbe is not only opening the door to the largest donations, but is making a powerful statement of confidence in every single Jew: that there exists the possibility to serve God in a perfect manner, beyond any upper limit.

---

15. *Likutei Sichos* (KPS, 1989), vol. 27, p. 17.

3

Existing on the Basis
of an Excuse

The audience gasped in amazement as the leading witness for the prosecution entered the packed courthouse. With large black hat, long black coat, and an even longer black beard, a Chassidic Jew was a most unlikely expert witness, and as he made his way toward the witness box, the clerk of the Court immediately called out for a "Yiddish interpreter."

An old man came from the back of the court claiming to speak Yiddish, and was consequently placed directly next to the Chassidic Jew. However, before the case could proceed, the witness announced a clear objection in beautifully-articulated English.

"Although I was born in Eastern Europe," began the Chassid, "I arrived in England at age three, and immediately entered one of the finest Preparatory schools in the country. I proceeded to spend ten glorious years at Eton and then graduated *summa cum laude* from Harvard, after which I undertook graduate studies at Yale and Stanford Universities in English Literature and Linguistics. I speak twenty-seven languages

fluently and have authored more than 100 works on
the English language. I do not therefore require a Yiddish interpreter."

Finally, as the Chassid concluded his lengthy objection, the Judge peered over his bench and inquired of
the Yiddish interpreter, "*Was sagst der Meshuganner?*"
("What did that fool just say?")

DRESSING THE PART

It is not only those who dress in the "orthodox garb"
who are expected to display specifically Jewish idiosyn-
crasies: it is anticipated that certain events will inspire
all Jews to respond in a quintessentially "Jewish" manner. All are expected to be charitable, and yet it is perhaps often the case that an individual can become so
immersed in his quest for money that he totally for-
gets his obligations as a Jew. Ultimately, he may be
willing to sacrifice any mitzvah for his work, on the
basis that "religion does not fill one's stomach."

One of the first mitzvahs to suffer in the struggle
for personal wealth is *tzedakah.* Although many Jews do
give considerable donations to charitable causes, there
is a minimum obligation in Jewish law of ten percent
(*maaser*). To many, this sum appears exorbitant and
unrealistic; yet ten percent is a Jew's absolute minimum obligation.[1] While the world of business permits
tzedakah donations from everybody, including the least
religious, it also discourages *maaser* donations as being
far too much money, even for the most religious.

It might seem that earning a living or having a
profession poses some contradiction to being a totally
committed Jew. The excessive energies that are de-

---

1. *Shulchan Aruch, Yoreh Deah,* 249:1.

manded of a person in order to earn a reasonable living are a major distraction from the observance of Torah and mitzvahs, and for this reason many people are tempted to think that a pious and meager life of prayer, Torah learning, and little work is the "ideal" existence for a religious Jew. Perhaps, work is only for those who lack faith.

However, Jewish thought instructs that "Through the toil of your hands, you will eat."[2] This signifies that the authentic Jewish view is that a livelihood does not come through simple piety, but must be earned through hard work. In fact, many of the greatest Torah sages throughout history had professions: the Rambam and the Ramban were both prolific doctors, and Rashi was a wine merchant. A profession is in no way a contradiction to faith in God, because a Jew has to believe that it is not through his own merit or through the actual work itself that his income arrives, but that it is the blessing of God, in the guise of nature.[3]

The world says that if you work harder and longer hours, you will earn more money, because everything is achieved by you and there is nobody else to help. Although this philosophy appears eminently reasonable, it ignores the fact that one's income is rarely commensurate with actual work-time and effort—"luck" often plays a major role in becoming rich. In fact, the billionaire J. Paul Getty suggested that his "formula for success is Rise early; Work late; Strike oil."

A Jew must work because the Torah says he must, and yet he must know that he only need carry out enough work to act as a sufficient vehicle, so that God can provide for him. This resolves the apparent problem that on the one hand "God provides everything,"

---

2. Ps. 128:2.
3. *Derech Mitzvosecha* 107a, 8a; *Kuntres Umayon* 25:1.

but on the other, He told us to work. The Midrash itself proves this to be the case, and states "Although you might think that a person could sit and be idle, the Torah says '[and your God will bless you] in all that you do.'"[4] Hence, the Torah itself instructs that a blessing from God will only come in response to the fact that a man goes to work.

However, why does a benevolent God expect a man to work so hard for a "blessing," a reward which the worker is not in fact earning himself? The truth is that God did not want it to be this way. He placed man in the Garden of Eden where no effort at all was required, and one of the consequences of the sin of the "Tree of Knowledge" was the need to work for a living. After the sin, God told Adam, "By the sweat of your brow, you will eat bread,"[5] as the world entered into a state where truth is not apparent and God's very presence became concealed.[6]

DON'T LOSE YOUR HEAD

The Alter Rebbe states in his classic work *Likutei Torah*,[7] that the command "through the toil of your hands, you shall eat" is not a general instruction to work, but a specific request that the "hands" should be used for this purpose, and not the brain or the heart. Some misinterpret this statement, citing it as a proof that it

---

4. Deut. 15:18; and *Sifri*, 15:18.

5. Gen. 3:19.

6. A Jew is not supposed to be content with this situation; in fact, most of the *amidah* prayer is devoted to requests that this state of affairs should finally end, as promised.

7. Num. 42d, 66c.

is a mitzvah to search for a profession which involves only manual labour, without any intellectual involvement whatsoever. They claim that this represents a prohibition upon using the mind for anything except Torah study, since man's highest faculties should be devoted to a meaningful occupation.

However, while it is true that a Jew should devote his mind to the study of Torah, the statement of the Alter Rebbe does not come to prohibit using one's brain for an occupation: every type of work requires concentration and some degree of intellect. The idea that one should use his "hands" and not his brain means that a person should not immerse his mind into his work more than is necessary. When he is away from the workplace he should not be constantly thinking of his business, when it is possible for him to occupy himself in more holy pursuits.[8]

The more a person is overwhelmed by his business and feels that his income rests upon his own shoulders, the more he will find an excuse not to give *tzedakah*. "I would love to give," a person may claim, "but I simply do not earn enough money." Such a person sees his financial shortcomings as his own fault, and genuinely would like to fulfil the mitzvah of *tzedakah*, but simply believes that he does not have sufficient skill to earn sufficient money. In truth, he should see his work as merely a "garment" to his earnings, rather than their actual source. If he appreciated that his income is really allocated by God, and his work is only making that blessing fit into the world[9] "like an arm

---

8. *Likutei Sichos*, 2nd ed., vol. 20 (KPS, 1989), pp. 276–277.

9. "It is the blessing of God that makes one rich"—Prov. 10:22.

in a shirt sleeve," then he would see his low income as a fact of life, rather than a personal failure.

TRYING TO OUTSMART GOD

"This is a particularly cheap suit," remarked the Jew, "but I am afraid I cannot take it because the left sleeve is longer than the right one."

"That's no problem," the shopkeeper replied, "Just lean a little to the left and nobody will ever notice."

"But if I do that," the Jew complained as he twisted his body sideways, "the right trouser leg sticks out."

"That's easy to correct," said the shopkeeper, "just bend your right knee as you walk and it will be unnoticeable."

"But the jacket is still much too big!"

"If you lean backwards," the shopkeeper explained, "the extra size will not show."

"OK, since it's so incredibly cheap, I'll take it," the Jew finally conceded. He left the store wearing his new suit and walked confidently down the street, with his body twisted in various directions.

"Look at that poor man!" remarked a passer-by to her husband, "He can barely walk."

"Yes," replied the husband, "but doesn't that suit fit him well!"

A garment has to fit the person. While a larger garment may boast more material and be a much better value for the money, when it is too large it appears unsightly and normal walking is difficult. Increasing a garment's size beyond the appropriate contradicts its entire purpose.

The Tzemach Tzedek (the third Lubavitcher Rebbe, 1789-1866) compared this principle in his *Book of*

Mitzvahs to the concept of working for a living: "A person who increases the size of his clothes gets no benefit at all, and to the contrary, it is a greater obstacle to him."[10] He explains that this is analogous to working, because a person's earnings are a sum decided by God, and the work which a person does is merely a garment in which to dress this money. Therefore, if a person works excessively, he will not automatically earn more money, and instead it could act as an obstacle to the Divine blessing of his earnings. In the same way that one's body is determined from above, and we simply look for clothes which fit, so too is one's wealth decided from above, and one's work should simply be a garment which will "fit" a predetermined body of money.[11]

---

10. *Derech Mitzvosecha* of the *Tzemach Tzedek* (KPS, 1993), p. 107b.

11. A garment "hides" the body that is beneath, so that when an arm is moved it superficially appears that it is the shirt which moves, while in fact it does nothing—the arm obviously moves the shirt. This is exactly the case with one's work, which "hides" the divine blessing of wealth. Superficially it appears that one's work achieves wealth, yet it is now understood that the work is simply the garment which "hides" the blessing. In a world where even God Himself is concealed, His role as the provider of all our needs is similarly hidden.

The analogy of the *Tzemach Tzedek* seems also to answer the logical question that if we cannot know precisely how much money has been predetermined for us (and thus cannot know how much money the laws of *tzedakah* will demand from us), how can we know what is the appropriate "garment" of work—how many hours is appropriate to earn our living? One could conjecture that in the same way that an item of clothing will look acceptable even if it is a little too small or too large, the hours one should work also have an element of leeway. Just don't be extreme: clothes

TROUBLED WATERS

One of the most famous of the twenty-four books of
the Bible is King Solomon's "Song of Songs," which
depicts the relationship between a Jew and God in
terms of the fiery love between man and woman. The
love between friends or family is a constant one, since

---

which are extremely small look stupid; likewise, barely
working makes no sense. Clothes that are much too large
defeat their own purpose, as does working excessively:
being a workaholic defeats the purpose of work.

Working for a living also effects a certain compatibil-
ity with one's environment. The same society which ex-
pects its citizens to wear clothing also regards working for
a living as fitting behavior. The modern world does not
suffer the lazy gladly, and deems him as almost similar to
the nudist—an unpleasant social aberration. This could also
be evidenced by the fact that just as before the sin of the
Tree of Knowledge, work was not required to achieve the
necessities of life, so too was the wearing of any clothing
not necessary for the inhabitants of the world. The "sin"
brought the need for both work and garments.

The Talmud (*Bava Basra* 9a) also compares *tzedakah*
to a garment of clothing, and suggests that "just as many
threads combine to make a garment, so do many small
amounts given to charity combine into one large amount."
The analogy also illustrates that *tzedakah* acts as a source
of protection for the giver, in a similar way that a garment
protects its wearer.

Ultimately, the *Tzemach Tzedek*'s analogy fits perfectly
the spiritual concept which it is explaining, because in
reality the physical world is a reflection of the spiritual
world. So when the *Tzemach Tzedek* offers a physical comparison, he is not merely concocting an analogy, but is
pointing out the physical entity which reflects the spiritual
state of affairs.

the relationship remains relatively stable over a long period, but the love between a man and woman is turbulent, fluctuating, and full of tension. As a Jew stands before God, he continually strives to draw closer to his Creator; but the love is tense, since there is a constant battle between feelings of surrender and selfishness.

In the course of this description, King Solomon proclaims, "Many waters cannot extinguish the love, and rivers cannot wash it away."[12] Chabad Chassidic philosophy explains that the "many waters" referred to in this verse represent "the stress of earning a living."[13] The verse offers encouragement to every Jew, by stating that however great the burden of earning money may be, it can never "extinguish" the hidden love which a Jew has for God. Even when financial problems reach the level of "rivers" which surge continuously, without interruption, this love is not "washed away."[14]

CONNECTING THE MYSTICAL
WITH THE MUNDANE

The requirement to earn a living is an observable reality, whereas "the hidden love for God" is a deep mystical truth. Nevertheless, by refusing to be affected by the rivers of materialism, the soul displays such a profound strength in its repulsion of the need to earn, that it actually affects the material world.

King Solomon, in revealing the inner identity of the soul, has provided a strong answer for those who claim that giving the required sum of ten percent (or

---

12. Song of Songs 8:7.
13. *Torah Ohr* 8c, beginning of *parshas Noach*.
14. *Toras Chayim* 62b.

more) to *tzedakah* is unrealistic. It is a simple fact that "Many waters cannot extinguish the love," meaning that however turbulent are one's financial difficulties, they cannot extinguish the intense yearning of the soul, and its insatiable love for the giving of *tzedakah*.

Since *tzedakah* "weighs against all mitzvahs,"[15] it is a major pathway for the love that a Jew has for God, expressed in practical acts. Consequently, charitable donations are a major target for disturbance by the "many waters" of the business world, and yet "the love" which a Jew has for the mitzvah of *tzedakah* can ultimately not be "washed away."

Nevertheless, two fundamental problems remain with this understanding. First, why is it that "Many waters cannot extinguish the love, and rivers cannot wash it away," when it is surely possible for any person to lose his own personal battle of performing the mitzvah of *tzedakah* (versus the stress of earning a living)? Secondly, it is apparent that many people do indeed lose their battles and succumb to the temptation to place their careers before their obligations as Jews, so how could the verse claim that this does not occur?

WHAT'S A NICE SOUL LIKE YOU DOING IN A BODY LIKE THIS?

It is known that the soul exists even before the birth of a person,[16] when it enters his body, to carry out the task of living within this world. Similarly, a Jew understands that after a person departs from this world, this does not represent his final end, but the soul ascends

---

15. *Bava Basra* 9a.
16. See *Bereishis Rabbah* 1:4.

back to Heaven, having benefitted from all the worthy acts which it performed when it was in a body below.[17]

While this classic idea is quite simple and satisfying, upon closer examination it does not appear to make any sense at all. When the soul is above, it is close to God, it is in a constant state of ecstasy; and it would seem totally unnecessary for it to descend into a physical body, which can only distance it from Godliness. The body itself is drawn toward material desire and selfishness, which is the very opposite of truth, and in order to have any notion of holiness requires a very great degree of effort.[18]

Furthermore, the descent of the soul into the body seems to be unreasonable, because the sheer delight and pleasure which is experienced above is far more exciting than anything obtainable on earth. This is attested to by the saying, "One hour of bliss in the world to come, is better than all of the life of this world."[19] The sheer pleasure of the soul, before it descends into the body, is incomparably greater than anything obtainable in the physical realms: What, therefore, did God have in mind when he created the human body?

TO HELP AN OLD LADY CROSS THE STREET

The answer to this question is one word: *Teshuvah*.[20] The only positive experience which cannot be enjoyed in heaven is overcoming a challenge, because for this

---

17. See *Torah Ohr* & *Toras Chayim*, ibid. *Or Ha'Torah*, *Noach*, vol. 3, p. 622a.
18. See *Derech Mitzvosecha*, *Maamar*, "*Pru U'rvu*."
19. *Pirkei Avos*, *Ethics of the Fathers*, 4:17.
20. See *Torah Ohr*, ibid., 9a. *Toras Chayim*, ibid., 59d.

to happen there has to be the possibility of failure. In a world of only souls, a world of truth, ordeals do not exist. Consequently, such a world lacks the opportunity for any real sense of accomplishment.

Teshuvah, according to its correct meaning, is not repentance but a *return* to truth.[21] Therefore, in order to acquire the great accomplishment of return, there first has to be an enforced distancing. For a soul to become separate from God is against its will, yet in the Divine plan God perceived that accomplishment and triumph from a situation of danger are ultimately more significant in a relationship than close-knit love. The real way for a Jew to become close to God is for him to show that his love remains just as strong, even at a distance.[22]

When the soul is above, it has a steady, intimate relationship with God,[23] but while this type of love is always strong, it lacks a certain excitement—the feeling of coming closer. This is similar to the love between brothers, which is enduring and profound, but not fiery. On the other hand, the love between a man and his wife may fluctuate wildly, but it is this very turbulence that provides the excitement.

God knows the very great sacrifices which the soul has to make upon its descent into the body, in terms of how close it is with its Creator. Nevertheless, the ultimate purpose of its descent is so that the soul should overcome its challenge and return to God, having rejected the distractions of the world.[24]

---

21. Tanya, *Iggeres HaTeshuvah*, ch. 1.

22. "In the place of those who have mastered *Teshuvah*, even the completely righteous cannot stand"—*Berachos* 34b.

23. *Likutei Torah, Balak* 73a.

24. For the following explanation, see *Sefer HaMaamorim, Meluket* 1 (KPS, 1993), p. 275.

The "many waters" which disturb a person from giving *tzedakah* are in fact the key "distancing factor" in God's plan. In order that a challenge should exist, God created the economic waters of temptation, so that a Jew should overcome them. This challenge is the justification for the soul leaving its heaven. The desire to earn money is of sufficient allurement to inspire neglect of mitzvahs, since the greater the challenge, the greater the achievement of the *teshuvah*. The reason that a person could be drawn away from Judaism to earn more money, is because the descent of the soul can only be justified if the potential for achievement is very great. For this to be so, the temptation must be equally strong.

It could never occur that the "many waters" of financial burden could cause an insurmountable obstacle to the observance of mitzvahs, because their very purpose is to provide a surmountable one. If a challenge is too difficult, it ceases to be a challenge, because there is no longer the potential for success. Therefore, when God created the "many waters" to disturb a Jew from his religious obligations, He only gave them sufficient strength to present a genuine challenge, rather than a dead end. On the other hand, He made them extremely powerful, so that the accomplishment of overcoming them would be great. So the "many waters" are incapable of extinguishing the hidden love which a Jew has for God, since a creation can never totally defeat its own purpose.

When a Jew is confronted with a challenge which seems to make him sacrifice a mitzvah in order to have more money, he must remember his soul. This challenge is part of a larger plan: "to open one's eyes" is the best source of encouragement to overcome the challenge.

There is a Chassidic dicta that "every descent is for the sake of an even greater ascent," and since a Jew believes that God is ultimately good, he knows that evil does not exist, except as a key to an even greater good. When a Jew is confronted by a dilemma, either to give the amount of *tzedakah* which the Torah requires of him or to allocate the money for other "needs," he should take a few moments to reflect—as soon as he recognizes that it is merely a test, he has already won.

4

Going Hungry
or Going Bankrupt

Judge Greenberg summed up the case most fairly, and then announced that he would give his judgment in this divorce litigation the following morning.

However, a mere five minutes after returning home, the Judge received a phone call from the husband in the case, who announced that there was $50,000, in a briefcase outside his front door, saying, "I look forward to tomorrow's good news." Judge Greenberg opened his front door and found exactly that sum awaiting him.

One hour passed, and a telephone call was received from the wife in the case. "There is $100,000 at the bottom of your garden," she said, "please remember this when you finally reach a decision." At the designated place, the judge found a large plastic bag filled with dollar bills.

The next morning, as the husband and wife stood before him in court, Judge Greenberg made an announcement. "Yesterday evening," he began, "Mr. Cohen left $50,000 outside my house as a bribe. He should know that I will not allow this act of dishonesty to influence my decision. One hour later, Mrs. Cohen placed $100,000 in my garden; I refuse to be corrupted by this sum, also."

"Consequently," concluded Judge Greenberg, "I intend to return to Mrs. Cohen the sum of $50,000, and then I can judge this case equally and fairly."

SINS FOR SALE

Although the famous adage suggests that "every person has his price," it could obviously not be said of God, who is ultimately fair, that a person could buy a favorable judgment by merely writing a large check. It therefore seems somewhat problematic that penitential fasts, which are necessary to atone for a variety of sins, can be "replaced" by charitable donations.[1] Surely this resembles, to a considerable extent, offering a "bribe" for one's misdeeds, since it is now possible through financial means to attain forgiveness. It conjures a rather disturbing picture of a wealthy Jew, who enjoys a luxurious lifestyle and is involved in activities of a dubious moral nature, but nevertheless achieves the heights of holiness through his large gifts to charity. Is this really Judaism, where favor in the eyes of God can be acquired for a price?

In earlier generations penitential fasting was widespread, as Jewish law recommends that a person should accept upon himself optional fasts as a means of ensuring forgiveness for his sins. However, compared to the giants of the past, the latest few generations in Jewish history are considered spiritual weaklings, so it is generally accepted that regular fasting is not consid-

---

1. See Tanya, *Iggeres HaTehuvah*, ch. 3.

ered viable as a mode of Divine service. This is simply because most people cannot take their minds off food when they are deprived of the opportunity to eat for more than a few hours. Since fasting is intended to achieve atonement for sins, it must be accompanied by an increased observance of Torah and mitzvot to achieve this goal. So if it instead leads to fatigue and longing for food, it is barely worthwhile taking upon oneself an optional fast,[2] since such behavior is unlikely to inspire any form of atonement.

Giving *tzedakah* is also considered a form of atonement, so in modern times there is no upper limit to one's donations to charity, because one's penitential fasts can be replaced by increasing *tzedakah*. Since charity is able to "buy back" fasts which are required to "save" our souls, there is no longer any limit to the amount one pays (see chapter 2, above).

SWAP-SHOP

One explanation as to why *tzedakah* is capable of "redeeming" the necessary fasts is to not consider it as a form of "Divine bribery," but rather as the replacing of one mitzvah with another. In his famous treatise *Iggeres HaTeshuvah* ("Letters on Repentance"), the Alter Rebbe enumerates exactly how many fasts are required to atone for various sins, and then proceeds to explain that these fasts can be exchanged for the alter-

---

2. This is clearly different from the compulsory fast days enumerated in the Jewish calendar, such as Yom Kippur and Tisha Ba'Av, in which "the day itself" has a specific power, and therefore even the weakest person benefits greatly from fasting on such days—these days cannot be "redeemed" by giving money to charity.

native mitzvah of *tzedakah*, based on the verse "Your sins are cast away through *tzedakah*."[3] Therefore, this is hardly a case of bribing God, but is actually the replacement of one form of Divine service with an appropriate alternative.

However, it is a simple fact that since the Torah has Divine authorship, any two concepts or activities which it connects must have more than an incidental similarity. In fact, they must, in essence, be the same. So when the Torah connects *tzedakah* with fasting and says that they are interchangeable, the reason for this must be that the function of *tzedakah* in the Divine Plan has a deep, intrinsic connection with the concept of a fast.

SUCH A THING AS A FREE LUNCH

A cursory glance at any Economics textbook will be repaid by the information that the financial world is ruled by the laws of supply and demand. The price we pay for any product is determined by how much the producers of that product are willing and able to supply, and how much the consumers are ready to demand it. At the "equilibrium" point, where the amount supplied equals the amount demanded, the price will be fixed. Thus, every financial transaction that occurs requires a supplier and a demander, or put more simply, a giver and a receiver.

The fact that the entire basis of world trade focuses on the relationship between "giver" and "receiver" is a natural consequence of the way in which God created the World. Every creature by necessity has to give and receive and cannot exist in isolation. Naturally, an

---

3. Dan. 4:24.

all-powerful God could have designed the world in any way that He wished. He could have made a world in which the inhabitants had no need to relate to each other, and no need to provide for each other in order to sustain their own existence or further their development. Instead, He chose to create a world of interdependent beings, who rely upon communication and mutual support as the basis of their lives.

For a Jew who believes in the perfection of the Divine Plan, the reason for which the world was designed in the manner of "give and take" is clear. A world in which individual creatures cannot live alone necessitates constant exchange between themselves. God made a world based upon "supply and demand" to ensure that for the world to remain in existence his creatures would be compelled to continually perform acts of *tzedakah*.[4]

Concerning this point, the Midrash records the response of God to a question of King David, who was perplexed as to why rich and poor had been created. God replied "If the whole world was rich or poor, how could kindness be performed?"[5] Clearly, the very possibility for kindness and charity only exists in a world of givers and receivers. To make the whole world wealthy would not represent an example of Divine benevolence, but rather the elimination of human benevolence, as charity can only occur in an "unfair" world.

Further evidence that *tzedakah* is intrinsic to the fabric of creation is the fact that *tzedakah* is one of the few mitzvahs that, if it had not been commanded in the Torah, would have still been carried out. The human intellect comprehends that it is necessary to aid others

---

4. *Siddur im D'ach* of the Alter Rebbe, 94:4.
5. *Shemos Rabbah* 31:5.

in such a profound way that it could even be argued that *tzedakah* is one of the most "obvious" mitzvahs in the Torah.[6]

From a broader perspective, the whole of creation could be collectively viewed as a recipient from God Himself, the ultimate giver of everything. In this way, the entire sustenance of the world can be seen as *tzedakah* from God, since there is no reason why God would have to sustain the world, and He does so purely through kindness.[7] All one's physical requirements for daily life can be considered gifts of charity from God, even the food that one eats.

WITH ALL HIS DOUGH

Having read much about the Temple of Solomon, the old Jewish lady decided that she wanted to follow the ancient practice of baking twelve loaves of bread and offering them to God. She therefore visited her local synagogue and placed twelve fresh loaves in the holy Ark, and was amazed to return one hour later to find that the Ark was empty, her offering having been accepted.

---

6. God made charity as a natural human emotion which is so basic that the Tanya (ch. 1) states that it can even be inspired by the "animalistic soul" of a Jew.

7. As it is written in the Grace after Meals that God "in His goodness, provides sustenance for the entire world with grace, with kindness, and with mercy." King David expresses the idea that God performs the mitzvah of *tzedakah* in psalm 119 (verse 96) with the words, "Your mitzvah is very broad," on which the commentators explain that this mitzvah is specifically that of *tzedakah* (*Iggeres Kodesh*, ch. 17).

Her delight was not, however, as great as that of the penniless Jewish beggar who had prayed with particular devotion that morning and who, even before he entered the synagogue for afternoon prayers, was overwhelmed by the most delightful smell. He opened the Ark, and was astonished by the literal "Divine gift" of more bread than he had ever seen before.

Each subsequent week, the old Jewish lady was elated that her twelve fresh loaves were continually accepted by God. Meanwhile, the penniless beggar was overjoyed by the vast quantity of fresh bread that God placed in the Ark for him, once a week.

However, on one occasion the penniless Jew arrived for the afternoon service early, and witnessed the old lady placing "her" fresh bread in the holy Ark; he was terribly upset and was unable to thank God in the afternoon service with the same devotion that he had felt when he had thought the bread was a Divine gift.

The mistake of the penniless Jew was that he failed to realize that the bread that he continually found in the Ark was actually the *tzedakah* of God, given to him through natural means. If the penniless Jew had known that all good things in life which appear to happen through natural means are really Divine *tzedakah*, then he would not have been surprised or disappointed when he saw the means by which the bread was put into the Ark—since it really did come from God, but through the hands of the old lady.

The Talmud[8] takes this idea a stage further and asserts that God is actually "inspired" to give *tzedakah* in greater proportions when he sees his creatures performing this mitzvah below. This means that as God decided that He would give *tzedakah* in response to our

---

8. *Sotah* 8b and 9b.

tzedakah, it became necessary to design a world in which acts of charity were continually occurring. It was only in this way that God's sustenance of the world could be inspired.

Since God's *tzedakah* depends upon our *tzedakah*, we must continually give to each other, in order that God should give to us. So, by implanting charity and kindness into the fabric of creation, God, so to speak, wrote an insurance policy which guaranteed a never-ending source for the arousal of His own mercy.[9]

TO FEED WITH HUNGER

Tzedakah, in whatever form it takes, is the basis of the functioning of the world. Not only do humans and animals support each other by constant acts of giving, but even God Himself is seen as a giver of charity, since all sustenance ultimately comes from Him. However, one problem arises with this explanation, since there are certain days in the year when Jews do not eat. Are we to assume that on a fast day, God decides to simply stop giving the *tzedakah* of food and sustenance? The bold statement that the entire world "continually" depends upon Divine *tzedakah* appears to ignore these very important days.

In the *siddur* of the Arizal[10] (Rabbi Issac Luria, 1534–1572), a novel explanation is found concerning physical sustenance on Yom Kippur. He explains that the hunger of this holy day is not the absence of sustenance but rather a higher level of food itself. Paradoxically,

---

9. *Sefer Hasichos* 5751/1991 (KPS, 1992), pp. 320–321.
10. *Gate of Kavanos*. See also Pri Etz Chayim, *Gate of Yom Kippur*, ch. 1; *Likutei Torah, Shir HaShirim* 14b; *Sefer HaMaamorim* 5564, p. 138.

hunger is seen to be more of a source of energy for the person than food, as the absence of food allows God to saturate the person with much more energy than would otherwise be possible. This theme is hinted to by King David in a verse at the end of psalm 33, which can be translated as "to feed them with hunger." Hence, the Arizal's message is that the fasting of Yom Kippur is, in truth, a greater source of energy than food.

There is a story of two Jews discussing the piety of their respective Rabbis. Each of the Jews produced evidence as to the great volume of learning and vast number of religious activities that each of their Rabbis were known to perform, until finally one Jew produced a proof that was unbeatable.

"My Rabbi," he boasted, "is so holy that last week when he was walking down the street in a big thunderstorm, he merely had to wave his hands and then in a little circle above his head the rain stopped and the sun shone through."

"That's nothing!" replied the second Jew. "My Rabbi could easily do that if he wanted to, he's just too modest."

"How can you say that," screamed the first Jew in disgust, "when it is well known that your Rabbi was seen eating a sandwich on Yom Kippur this year!"

"That's because he merely had to wave his hands," pronounced the second Jew proudly, "and then in a little circle above his head it was the day after Yom Kippur!"

However holy a man is, even if he can work miracles, it is still not a good idea to eat on Yom Kippur. Even if the story of the second rabbi were true, it is not a satisfactory situation because not eating on a fast day achieves far more than eating on the day after.

In a simple sense, many people feel that "clearing-out" the body of food for a day is good for the health, but such a sentiment is really a consequence of a deeper truth. Chassidic thought explains the Arizal's comment that the starvation of a fast day is a greater source of energy than food not as deep mysticism, but as reasoned observation.

IT'S A REAL PLEASURE

In the vast array of experiences that life has to offer there are two types of pleasure. The first level is pleasure that can be felt and enjoyed, but this does not necessarily mean that the pleasure is physical: it could be intellectual, musical, aesthetic, or simple beauty, so long as it gives the person an essential delight whenever it is experienced.

Chassidic thought explains that there is a second, much more sublime level of pleasure, "pleasure that cannot be felt." This pleasure is of such a high level that it does not satisfy the senses of a person, but satisfies the very essence of a person—the essence which transcends his consciousness.[11] An example of this is the simple pleasure to be alive that cannot be felt yet is the greatest joy a person can have. In fact, the only occasion when a person actually has a sensation of this pleasure is when he is close to death, when the pleasure is at risk; only then does he have some kind of perception as to what a joy it really is to be alive. It is rather like the exhilaration of the rollercoaster, which brings the person to a point when he begins to taste that level of pleasure.

---

11. See *Hemshech Yom-Tov shel Rosh-Hashanah 5666, Vayere-Vayishlach.*

The tragedy of those who lose their lives through smoking or eating to excess illustrates precisely this distinction. Another cigarette or steak provides pleasure that can be felt, but the mistake is that it can cause the loss of a much greater pleasure, that of life itself. It is very easy to make such a mistake because this highest level of pleasure simply cannot be sensed.[12]

It is this most lofty level of pleasure that is given to a person on Yom Kippur, as a gift from God. The inner reason for fasting is that the pleasure a Jew has on this day is much higher than the pleasure from food. In fact, it is so high that it hits the very essence of the person, where sensation cannot reach.

The *tzedakah* that God performs on a fast day is therefore far greater than the *tzedakah* He gives on other days. During the rest of the year God provides food for us on a daily basis which keeps us alive, but on fast days he gives us an energy that is the power of living. This is a pleasure that cannot be felt because it reaches the essence of a person, in a similar sense to the way that one does not feel continually happy to be alive.

THE SAME AROUSAL

The inner connection between fasting and charitable donations can now be understood. The common link which these two activities share is that they are both the means by which a Jew can arouse his Creator to shower a flow of additional energy and sustenance upon him: they both inspire God to give *tzedakah*.

---

12. The comparison between "Pleasure that cannot be felt" and the "Pleasure of being alive" was heard by the authors from HaRav Yosef Greenberg Shlita.

Tzedakah achieves this goal, because according to the design of creation, God decided that He would give *tzedakah* in response to the charity of man. Therefore, when a Jew gives *tzedakah*, it is a key influencing factor in God's decision to grant the Jew sustenance and life. Similarly, a fast achieves the same goal, since it is explained by the Arizal to be a deeper and more potent source of sustenance than food itself, because it is a pleasure which cannot be felt. Therefore fasting also causes an arousal of a great *tzedakah* by God, which takes the form of a shower of energy and life.[13]

The deeper reason why a fast can be redeemed by *tzedakah* is, therefore, because in essence a fast achieves exactly the same results as giving to *tzedakah*: They are both pathways to inspiring Divine charity. For this reason, in the current era, where fasting is largely inappropriate, *tzedakah* is of heightened importance, and should be given in unprecedented proportions.

---

13. See footnote 32 of *Sefer Hasichos* 5751, vol. 1 (KPS, 1992), p. 321. This footnote is the principle source for this chapter.

5

The Rich Go to Heaven

"If money is the world's curse . . . may the Lord smite me with it, and may I never recover." So says the hero of *Fiddler on the Roof*, before listing the aspirations and dreams which are only possible "If I were a rich man." Tevye the milkman craves the honor that society awards those who are financially prosperous ("if you're rich, they think you really know"); and while he inhabits a village which has few wealthy people to admire, those societies which boast much money are invariably greater respecters of the rich. Most modern ethics would suggest this should not be the case, and a man should not be judged by the size of his wallet. Jewish thought, however, does not entirely agree.

Due to the influence of much of the philosophy espoused in the Age of the Enlightenment, the writings of Karl Marx, and the theory of the modern Welfare State, the world today often appears predicated on the belief that money is some form of curse and that the wealthy are inherently evil. Such ideas are rooted in the inaccurate belief that for the rich to find favor in God's eyes and subsequently enter heaven is about as easy as "a camel passing through the eye of a needle." Judaism is unlike other -isms which tend to denigrate the physical and material while stumbling towards their own perception of the spiritual, as Jewish thought sincerely and practically recognizes the value of money and the onerous obligation which it brings (and Tevye perhaps overlooks).

"Rebbe" (R. Yehuda Hanasi, "the prince" and leader of the Jews from 170–200 C.E., compiler of the Mishnah, the essence of the oral law) was exceptionally well-known for the great honor that he extended toward the rich.[1] It appears strange for such a lofty and learned sage to be preoccupied with something so mundane as personal finance, and it must surely be the case that "Rebbe" 's admiration could only be based on the purest of motives. On a simple level, "Rebbe" honored the rich for their capacity to give substantial sums to charity. Although a poor man finds his "ten percent" more difficult to part with from the perspective of his needs, it is the rich whose donations not only have the greatest effect, but also are more subjectively difficult to part with.

However, the fact that "Rebbe" went out of his way to confer such considerable honor on the wealthy requires deeper analysis, and necessitates an understanding of the classic question of why the distinctions between "rich" and "poor" exist at all. If God is Just and He "sustains the whole world with his kindness," why doesn't he distribute wealth more equitably?

---

1. *Eruvin* 86a.

TO HELP A NAUGHTY PRINCE

The question was asked of Rabbi Akiva by Turnus Rufus, the Heretic,[2] "If your God loves poor people so much, why doesn't he feed them?" Turnus Rufus was not only wealthy and arrogant, but felt that he was personally worthy of his great riches, and consequently calculated that it was unnecessary to distribute charity.

Rabbi Akiva responded with an answer of great profundity, which ultimately justifies the "injustice" of poverty. He stated that God refrains from feeding the poor, "in order to give all of us the opportunity to fulfil the mitzvah of *tzedakah* ... and consequently save ourselves from the judgment of *Gehinom* [Hell]." Rabbi Akiva advocated the philosophy that *tzedakah* is a mitzvah, so cherished by the Almighty that He is prepared to witness the suffering of some of his creatures in order to facilitate its performance.

"A king became angry with his servant," responded Turnus Rufus, "and locked him in a prison; commanding that nobody bring any food to him. One person, however, fed the servant, and when the King heard of this disobedience, he understandably became angered." Since the Jewish people are referred to as "the *servants* of God,"[3] Turnus Rufus argues that "If God has decreed that a man be poor, how can one justify feeding him?" So Turnus Rufus not only rejects charity as a worthwhile occupation, but also suggests that rather than saving a Jew from *Gehinom*, it is through giving *tzedakah* that one actually "brings the judgment of *Gehinom* upon himself."

---

2. *Bava Basra* 10a.
3. Lev. 25:55.

Rather than being praised as "the pre-eminent mitzvah," *tzedakah* is condemned by this analogy as the ultimate denial of God's volition and a grave sin which merits "the judgment of *Gehinom*." If it is God's desire that a man be hungry or poor, the heretic advocates an approach which denounces the human intervention of *tzedakah* as a reversal of, and an affront to, the will of the King of Kings.

There is clearly a flaw in any assertion that *tzedakah* is not a mitzvah, and Rabbi Akiva proved himself an expert debater by refuting the heretics analogy with one of his own. He prefers the Jewish people's relationship as "*children* to God,"[4] and with this simple change in kinship is able to transform Turnus Rufus's own analogy into a powerful statement in favor of *tzedakah*.[5]

"A King became angry with his son," countered Rabbi Akiva, "and locked him in a prison; commanding that nobody bring any food to him. One person, however, fed the son, and when the King heard of this disobedience, did he not send gifts to the one who looked after his son?"

Tzedakah is thus transformed by Rabbi Akiva from an act of "civilized disobedience" to "a source of Divine delight." Although poverty, under certain circumstances, may be some form of punishment, wealth should not be viewed as a corollary reward, but as an

---

4. Deut. 14:1.

5. This relationship is beautifully emphasized by the Chief Rabbi of the United Kingdom, Jonathan Sacks, in his excellent series of essays, *Faith in the Future* (London: Dartman, Longman & Todd, 1995, p. 29), where he writes "Stephen Hawking was wrong in his *A Brief History of Time*. It is not through theoretical physics that we will approach an understanding of the 'mind of God.' It is through the feeling we have when we watch our children playing and they are unaware that we are watching them."

urgent obligation, since God gets considerable pleasure when *tzedakah* is given, even if the poverty of the
beneficiary was intended as a punishment. God ultimately distributed wealth unequally in order "to give
to the rich the opportunity to give to the poor."

THE WEALTHY MESSENGER

In his Grace after Meals, a Jew affirms that "God feeds
the whole world." Consequently, the food which a
wealthy man may give to his poor neighbor is actually
from God, and the rich man is simply "God's Messenger." The "charitable contribution" of the wealthy was
always the property of the poor man, and was simply
given to the rich "on deposit."

Yet, the rich ultimately deserve honor, not simply
because they have been chosen as *emissaries* for the
redistribution of wealth by God Himself, but actually
because of the enormous obstacles which they must
surmount in order to carry out such a mission. Although the incredible honor and profound duty of
being a "messenger of God" should make *tzedakah* a
relatively simple mitzvah to perform, there are two
major hurdles to overcome: the external obstacle of the
modern world which we inhabit, and the internal
obstacle of the human psyche. These two greatly ob-
scure the obvious merits of giving charity, and consequently being rich is a major test.

THE EXTERNAL OBSTACLE—LIVING
IN A MATERIAL WORLD

The first difficulty in the performance of the mitzvah
of *tzedakah* is reconciling a timeless obligation in a con-

stantly changing world. In order to become wealthy,
one must generally be involved in the world of business and commerce; however, this field demands
enterprise and innovation, which is often rooted in
self-advancement and common greed. Having succeeded in this area, the wealthy are then expected to
change their very nature, which may have been the
foundation of their achievements, and remind themselves that all their wealth (irrespective of how hard
they worked for it) is a "gift from God" and carries
with it a considerable obligation. There is thus a profound conflict of interest between one's responsi-
bilities as an entrepreneur and one's duties as a Jew.
Despite the incredible rewards for *tzedakah*, the test
of wealth does not appear as simple as Tevye perceived it to be.

THE POWER OF A FEAST

The story of Queen Esther and how she and her cousin
Mordechai saved the Jews from the decree of annihilation inspired by the evil prime minister Haman is
well known. The *Megillah* which narrates the events in
ancient Persia describes a feast which Esther's husband, King Ahashverosh, prepared for both Mordechai
and Haman, and states "the King had decided to do the
will of each person."[6] King Ahashverosh wanted to
please Mordechai and Haman at his feast.[7] When one
considers that Haman's aim was to kill all the Jews in
Persia and beyond, and Mordechai was devoted to the

---

6. Esther 1:8.
7. *Megillah* 12a.

thwarting of this plan, the King's desire to please both appears impossible.

The commentaries on the story of Esther offer two conflicting opinions as to whether the King could succeed in his plan to be "all things to all men."[8] The first opinion advocates that if two individuals represent completely opposing approaches to life, it is totally impossible to simultaneously reconcile their divergent desires. Since Mordechai's aim was to destroy Haman's plan, it is clearly not possible for the King to "do the will of each person."[9] However, the second commentary on this verse accepts the impossibility of such a desire in the present world, but argues that such seeming paradoxes will be reconciled in the Messianic era.[10]

According to the Midrash, Mordechai represents the Jewish approach to life, while Haman represents the opposite—the materialistic desires which challenge all things Jewish. Therefore, one appears to derive the rather uninspiring lesson that it is impossible to reconcile one's Jewishness (Mordechai) while remaining a part of the material world (Haman). Yet this cannot be the case, as it has already been observed that those who live and work in the material world are still expected to fulfil their Jewish obligations, particularly that of being God's emissary to the poor. Is this really fair when one appears to have only the freedom to choose either the materialistic or the Jewish, but not both?

---

8. Midrash *Esther*, ch. 2:4, and *Yalkut Shimoni* 247, 1048.

9. *Pirush Yafa Anaf Hashalem* on Esther.

10. According to Rav Huna in the name of Rav Benyamin ben Levi.

FREE TO CHOOSE

The Rambam writes, "Free will is granted to all men. If one wishes to pursue the path of good . . . the choice is his . . . man can of his own initiative . . . know good and evil and do as he wishes."[11] At the level where reconciling the material with the Jewish is impossible, our own free will determines which path is taken. The choice exists between involvement in the coarse and mundane material world or involvement in study of Jewish law and observance of such laws (and one is encouraged to derive inspiration from Mordechai, who would "neither bend the knee nor bow down").[12] Despite the pressures of the world, a Jew is expected to rise above worldly matters to study and fulfil the Divine will. Yet one who chooses spirituality and Torah has had minimal effect on the world around him, as he has failed to reconcile Judaism and materialism, *tzedakah* and commerce. He may not be controlled by the material aspects of his environment, yet he has had no influence upon them, either.

A deeper perspective is advanced by the second commentary, suggesting a reconciliation in the Messianic era of Mordechai (the performance of the mitzvah of *tzedakah*) and Haman (the world as a barrier to the fulfilment of this *tzedakah*). However, one need not necessarily wait until this era in order to satisfy both Mordechai and Haman simultaneously, to live in the material world and yet appreciate that it is not separate from God and His Torah. This is achieved today by "*appreciating the spiritual nature of material reality*,"[13] which occurs when a rich man makes a dona-

---

11. Rambam, *Hilchos Teshuvah*, ch. 5, 1–2.
12. Esther 3:2.
13. *Sefer Hasichos*, 5752/1992, vol. 1 (KPS, 1993), p. 221.

tion to *tzedakah* and accepts that all his involvement and hard work in the physical world was for the sake of this mitzvah.

The Jew is obliged to appreciate that the spiritual nature of the material reality of his business life is *tzedakah*. The big test is to not be fooled by one's own efforts in the world, and not to have thoughts that the material money earned is separate from the spiritual mitzvah to give.

THE INTERNAL OBSTACLE—THE MOST EXPENSIVE FRUIT EVER

An additional obstacle against giving *tzedakah*, and one which if surmounted merits much approbation, is the very nature of the human psyche: one's natural inclination toward the self, and away from the command to give charity.

The human body is like "a small city"[14] in which two inclinations are constantly at battle. When the rich succeed in their task as "messengers" of God, they are successfully conquering and winning the war against the inclination which advocates self-interest. So, while small donations from wealthy individuals are merely Pyrrhic victories against an evil inclination, a true emissary of the Divine enjoys a military triumph when he donates an appropriate amount.

The principal internal obstacle to giving *tzedakah* is the entity known as the "evil inclination." The real claim to fame and most substantial achievement of this entity occurred in the Garden of Eden, when Adam heard the prohibition concerning the Tree of Knowl-

---

14. Tanya, *Likutei Amarim*, ch. 11.

edge directly from God Himself and yet failed in a
seemingly simple act of self-restraint.[15] The answer to
the classic question as to how Adam could come to
transgress such an easy rule is explained by the existence of his "evil inclination."

All the different reasons which one's evil inclination proffers as to why one should or should not act in
a certain way derive from one single motive: that one
should transgress the will of God.[16] When a certain
commandment takes on a special importance (such as
the prohibition of the fruit in Eden, or the requirement
of the millionaire's donation to charity), the evil inclination makes a special effort to present various different demands and rationales which have the express
intent of preventing the individual from performing
the will of God.[17] Therefore, in the war which tran-
spires throughout one's body, the enemy within does
not fight consistently, but rather saves its strength for
those situations which it perceives to be the greatest
challenges.[18]

It is explained in the Talmud that "Whenever a
person is greater than a colleague, his evil inclination
is greater than he is."[19] So that although the poor man
has the greater need for every last penny, the millionaire has a more difficult battle with a substantially
more powerful evil inclination.

------

15. This is particularly so, when one considers that the
rule against eating from this one tree was to be lifted three
hours later, at the onset of the Sabbath—*Sanhedrin* 38b.

16. *Likutei Sichos*, vol. 3 (KPS, 1991), p. 747.

17. *Likutei Dibburim*, 19th Kislev 1932, ch. 5 (KPS, 1973),
p. 29.

18. *Sanhedrin* 97a.

19. *Sukkah* 52a.

NOT ALL IN THE SAME BOAT

There is a true story concerning a multimillionaire philanthropist who would pray every morning, even when he was travelling on his yacht. In order to fulfil the obligation to pray toward Jerusalem, the millionaire would continually ask the yacht's captain, "Which way is East?"

Ultimately, the Captain could not contain his curiosity as to why his boss showed only this minimal interest in the yacht's voyaging, and asked the purpose of this daily questioning. When he discovered that "even multimillionaires pray to God," and it is not merely the poor and desperate who beseech their Creator, the captain was overwhelmed.

"Rebbe" gave honor to the rich, not simply because they face a very difficult test and an awesome responsibility as *Messengers of God's will*, for the fact that someone's job is arduous is not automatic grounds for admiration. Respect for the rich is based on a simple rule in Judaism that "One is capable of fulfilling all the tests which God sends."[20] Thus, an individual who faces particularly difficult tests throughout his life is deemed by God to be an especially strong person. The test of wealth has been labelled "difficult"—based upon external and internal obstacles—and since all tests are within the ability of the person being tested, it logically follows that the wealthy have been deemed by God as able to endure this extremely difficult test.[21] This illustrates a high spiritual level on the part of the rich, and is the justification for "Rebbe"'s respect for them.

---

20. *Avodah Zorah* 3a.
21. *Sefer HaMaamorim*, Yiddish (KPS, 1986), p. 1.

Consequently, when a wealthy Jew meets the challenge of his task as the messenger of redistribution and the emissary of God's will, he will not only receive the reward for the mitzvah of *tzedakah*, but will also merit honor for withstanding the temptation and the clarion cry of the evil inclination to not give quite so much. Tevye may yearn for the honor which would follow "If I was a rich man," but he may not quite have appreciated that while Jewish thought encourages such respect for the wealthy, it is not based on actual success in the preceding acquisition, but rather expected success in the forthcoming obligation.

6

With All Your Might

There was an old English highwayman whose infamous greeting before robbing his victims was "Your money or your life!" However, faced with this rather unpleasant proposition, the wealthy Jew remained silent.

"I said, 'Your money or your life!'" the highwayman shouted, brandishing his pistol—but to no avail, as the Jew remained firm. Finally, the highwayman lost all patience and lifted the pistol to the Jew's head, ready to fire.

"This is your last chance . . . YOUR MONEY OR YOUR LIFE!"

"Please mister, give me a moment," complained the Jew, "I'm still thinking."

The "element of sacrifice" is a crucial component in the mitzvah of *tzedakah*. There have always been individuals who consider their money as their major priority and find it difficult to give "according to their means." For some, charitable donations of eighteen

dollars may constitute self-sacrifice, because this is
more than they can bear to give; for others, $18,000
may be an inconsiderable sum. Consequently, to make
a charitable donation "with self-sacrifice" is an activity
that is commensurate with one's financial capacity as
well as one's natural generosity, and is also a legal
obligation upon every individual.

This is illustrated by the Talmudic story of Nakdimon Ben Guryon, an exceptionally wealthy man
who would walk from his house to the synagogue
"with woollen clothes beneath his feet, and as he proceeded, the poor would follow behind and pick them
up [for themselves]."[1] This "donation" was not deemed
a fitting *tzedakah* since "he did not act in an appropriate manner—as it is said, 'according to the camel is the
burden.'" Nakdimon Ben Guryon did not give in ac-
cordance with his means. Thus, his gifts do not appear
able to boast the quality of sacrifice. To give *tzedakah*
with the appropriate degree of "self-sacrifice" appears
a rather lofty obligation.

"SET A PRECEDENT, PLEASE!"

For a deeper understanding of authentic self-sacrifice,
it is necessary to look back in Jewish history to the classic
episode of the *Akeidah*—the binding of Isaac. God's request to Abraham to sacrifice his only son on an altar
has captured the religious imagination, and its theme
is so central to Judaism that the Sages included it as the
introduction to the daily prayers. The *Akeidah* was the
last of ten trials with which Abraham was tested[2] during

---

1. *Kesubos* 66b.
2. *Avos* 5:3.

a life in which he struggled relentlessly to publicize the unity of God.

God's request was startling in both content and delivery. *"Please* take your son, your only son, whom you love . . . and offer him as a burnt offering."[3] The Talmud explains the word *please* carries with it the implication that, "I have tested you with many trials and you have withstood them all. Now, *please* succeed for My sake in this trial, so that the World cannot say that your earlier trials were worthless."[4]

The nine trials which preceded the *Akeidah* were challenges that had been unprecedented in human history. Abraham was a publicity-seeker: not for personal fame, but for the spreading of monotheism. Consequently, each of the preceding trials had been successful in displaying Abraham's absolute faith in the One True God.

Everything positive that Abraham stood for was embodied in the nine trials, and they were acts of immense bravery and incredible faith. It seems amazing that a failure to sacrifice his son, to fulfil the tenth test, would have nullified the earlier nine. Could it not simply mean that his capacity for self-sacrifice was not commensurate with this particular challenge?[5] There appears no logical explanation as to why Abraham's entire reputation would be obliterated by any lack of enthusiasm to kill his son.

Also, what is the unique feature of this trial that would not only have nullified that which preceded it,

---

3. Gen. 22:2.

4. *Sanhedrin* 99b.

5. *Sefer HaMaamorim, Kuntresim B*, 5th ed. (KPS, 1985), p. 642. For analysis of unique characteristics of the *Akeidah* from the perspective of Abraham's natural disposition.

but which results in Abraham's reputation for a degree of self-sacrifice which is incomparable to any act of sacrifice that came after it?

NOT SO SPECIAL!

When one takes into consideration that God made His request by speaking directly to Abraham, this test can surely not be compared to the countless acts of martyrdom of the last 4,000 years in which the Name of God was sanctified but the Voice of God was not heard. The specific request to sacrifice one's son when the words come directly from the Mouth of God cannot, at first glance, be compared to the incredible suffering and martyrdom of Rabbi Akiva, whose skin was scraped from his body with metal combs and yet who left this world with a smile and the words "*Shema Yisroel*" on his lips.

Although Abraham's test was more difficult than Rabbi Akiva's, in the sense that Abraham was not asked to sacrifice himself, but to sacrifice his son, the *Akeidah* is not unique in that sense. The harrowing story of Hannah and her sons portrays a mother forced to watch the murder of all her seven sons. Finally, as the seventh and smallest son was being led to his death, Hannah begged for the opportunity to kiss him "good-bye." She bent over to her son and whispered that he should tell his father, Abraham in Heaven, that "You [Abraham] sacrificed one son, and I [Hannah] sacrifice seven."[6]

There are also countless episodes during the Holocaust in which individuals were forced to watch the massacre of their entire families and communities, or

---

6. *Gittin* 57b.

walked into gas-chambers proclaiming the One-ness of God and their belief in the imminence of the coming of *Moshiach* (the Messiah). None of these individuals had the honor of a direct conversation with the Almighty. The entire history of the Jewish people is filled with tragedy and self-sacrifice and it is therefore difficult to appreciate the uniqueness of the sacrificing of Isaac.[7]

---

7. An answer is given to the absolute uniqueness of the *Akeidah* in the philosophical work the *Ikkarim* (R. Yosef Albo, 1357–1445). It suggests that the reason the *Akeidah* is invoked in the daily prayers and perceived as the ultimate in self-sacrifice is simply because Abraham had the complete freedom to choose whether or not to undertake God's request. There is absolutely no element of coercion or necessity in a statement that begins with "please sacrifice your son." The word "please" is the antithesis of a command, and clearly gives Abraham the opportunity to decline. It is also clear that even if Abraham was on such a level that he did not wish to decline even a request of the Creator, he still had the opportunity to present a perfect rebuttal to such a request. Earlier, God had said to Abraham "Through Isaac your descendants will be called," and therefore asking for the sacrificing of Isaac clearly contradicts one of God's earlier promises. It is evident that the word "please" and this clear escape clause, through a seeming Godly contradiction, elevates the *Akeidah* into a test which Abraham was entirely free to accept or reject.

However, this does not apply to the martyrs throughout Jewish history whose heroism and love of God inspired acts that were in total compliance with God's command, "and I shall be sanctified amidst the children of Israel" (*Emor* 22:32). These martyrs achieved the sanctification of God's name via their deaths, and thus performed a mitzvah—a divine command. The uniqueness of the *Akeidah* is thus in its total lack of any command or

TURNING ON THE TAP

Reb Yosef of Caro (1488-1575), the author of the Code of Jewish law, once encountered a particular difficulty in understanding a principle in Jewish law. After a lengthy period of concentrated study and intense intellectual application by this legal genius, he was still unable to find a satisfactory solution. When the answer

---

obligation, and in Abraham's willingness to do that which he need not do.

Nevertheless, this approach of the *Ikkarim* has two serious difficulties. To suggest, firstly, that Abraham had absolute freedom of choice, and secondly, that the other sacred martyrs were under a Divine obligation is not entirely correct—on both counts. Although God clearly uses the word "please," which implies the opportunity to decline, and although Abraham had a valid rationale for not sacrificing his son, when God Himself requests something, it is self-evidently obligatory. A request from the Almighty Himself, irrespective of the opportunity to decline (based on the nature of the request or a perfect excuse), is simply a thing that one does not fail to undertake.

Also, to suggest, concerning the martyrdom of the later generations, that their heroism was entirely due to an obligation or command, is wholly erroneous. On the contrary, it is difficult to find a legal justification to overrule the law that a person should "sin rather than be killed." It is a perversion of Jewish values to dismiss centuries of suffering and immense bravery as a mere compliance with one particular law. In most cases these martyrs were not obligated to give up their lives and their act was based on simple faith and an insatiable love of God. In reality, Rabbi Akiva chose the path of self-sacrifice without any obligation or direct request from God. This is not so with Abraham, who surely had as little choice as any other individual who receives a direct and specific request from the Almighty Himself.

was finally found, his relief was considerable, as it was rare that such a mind could be troubled for so long and experience such difficulty.

Shortly afterwards, Reb Yosef visited a synagogue where he happened to overhear two peasants discussing the very same point of law. His amazement increased upon hearing one of the peasants posing exactly the same question as the one that he had troubled over for so long. However this was minimal compared to his utter astonishment when he witnessed the second peasant glance briefly into a book before suggesting exactly the same answer that was the product of so much of Reb Yosef's time and genius. Unabashed, the peasants continued to learn.

Reb Yosef immediately sought the advice of his Rebbe the saintly Arizal as to how he could better utilize his time and brain for the benefit of the Jewish people. The Arizal explained that before Reb Yosef had solved this particular problem, the answer did not exist in the realm of intellect but only in its spiritual source. Through the power of Reb Yosef's mind and his faithful study, he was successful in making the answer understandable to the human mind, by bringing it from the potential into the actual. The Arizal concluded that, subsequent to Reb Yosef's profound innovation, it was now possible for anybody to understand this question and find its solution.

It was the same for Abraham at the *Akeidah*. He successfully opened the channel for the capacity to be a martyr, and his actions were the conduit for all subsequent acts of self sacrifice.[8] In the same way that Reb Yosef toiled in order to bring his answer down into the world, Abraham's actions at the *Akeidah* were the precedent from which all other acts of martyrdom pro-

---

8. *Likutei Sichos*, vol. 20, 2nd ed. (KPS, 1989), p. 77.

ceeded. The uniqueness of the *Akeidah*, according to Chassidic thought, is that Abraham was the first person who exemplified complete self-sacrifice. Its achievement is emphasized in the words of the sages "All beginnings are difficult."[9]

"GUNFIGHT!"

Nevertheless, there appears one outstanding difficulty with this answer: the *Akeidah* was not Abraham's first act of self-sacrifice. Prior to the *Akeidah* Abraham had to undergo his first test at Ur Kasdim, and subsequently underwent eight other trials before the *Akeidah*. At Ur Kasdim, Abraham risked his life in a place of idolatry in order to publicize the unity of God and eradicate idolatry from the world. This test demanded an unprecedented level of self-sacrifice. It could even be argued that the trial at Ur Kasdim, the first of the nine tests, was an even bigger act of self-sacrifice than the *Akeidah*, since God had not spoken directly to Abraham and commanded him to undertake and succeed in this activity.

This "difficulty" with the Chassidic solution is in fact a minor one and arises only through a lack of understanding of what "self-sacrifice" actually means. In Classical Hebrew, the term for self-sacrifice is *Messiras Nefesh*, which translates more precisely as "relinquishing the soul." This means that the entire make-up of the individual, his conscious faculties, emotions, and intellect, are returned to their Creator. In a more simple sense, it is the eradication of the ego, the source of all self-importance, as a result of pure submission to the Supreme Being.

---

9. Mechilta and Rashi, *Yisro* 19:5, and *Taanis* 10b.

₰ It is well known that the central tenet of Judaism is the *belief* in One God, but it is a very common mistake to suppose that the opposite of belief in God is atheism. Clearly, the opposite of any human emotion must be the reverse emotion, and atheism is not the opposite of belief, but merely the *absence* of belief. The opposite of belief in God is not atheism, but arrogance—an emotion that antagonizes and leaves no room for belief.

An atheist may be a "moral" person interested in the welfare of others; but an arrogant person is like a "sealed entity" who only participates in relationships as they might help him. It is for this reason that the Torah states that arrogance is worse than idolatry, since at least the idolater recognizes that there is something else in the universe besides himself.

This theme is expressed by the catch-phrase of the western cowboy, who on producing his gun would threaten, "This town ain't big enough for the both of us." Here, the cowboy is not perturbed by the presence of an adversary, but rather of another ego. Any town can easily support two inhabitants, but it cannot contain two egotists who each desire complete dominion.

Thus, self-sacrifice can only be accomplished through the complete elimination of the ego—in effect, the achievement of complete faith in God. Since all human beings are inherently steeped in self-awareness, self-sacrifice is the exact opposite of one's natural disposition. This is expressed in the Talmudic dictum that "A prisoner cannot free himself from his own imprisonment." Every individual is imprisoned by his ego, and its relinquishment would appear impossible. This is precisely how Chassidic philosophy explains Abraham's opening of the "pipe" of self-sacrifice, that he brought down self-sacrifice from the realm of the impossible to that of the possible. Abraham fitted the

ego with a "self-destruct button," so that, if there arose
a situation where a person could simply not serve God
because his ego proved to be an insurmountable obstacle, it would now be possible to dispose of it.

The uniqueness of the *Akeidah* was that it illustrated, for the first time, this ultimate in self-sacrifice.
Although the test at Ur Kasdim and the eight tests that
followed were unprecedented illustrations of heroism
and faith, it is possible to conceive of Abraham's motivation as a desire to promulgate monotheism, and although they had sanctity as their foundation, they
were intellectual and rational acts. The *Akeidah* exem-
plifies pure self-sacrifice, in that Abraham personified
faith beyond reason.

Therefore, the *Akeidah* sheds light retrospectively
upon the test at Ur Kasdim and all eight other ordeals,
and proves that they *were* rooted in authentic self-
sacrifice. This is how the Talmud explains God's use
of the word *please* "in case the world deems the previous test of no true significance." If not for the *Akeidah,*
it could have been argued that the previous test was
intellectually based, and therefore tarnished by the
ego. Retrospectively, the *Akeidah* elevates everything
that Abraham had achieved to the level of true self-
sacrifice.

A TOTALLY UNREASONABLE REQUEST

The foundation of all legal systems is the rule of precedent. Any decision can be made, but not for the first
time, and any legal argument requires the evidence of
a preceding judgment in order to substantiate its
validity. From the American Supreme Court to the
English House of Lords, the cases which provoke the
most effort and interest are those which set a prece-

dent. The precedent-setting case is the conduit for hundreds of subsequent judgments.

However, the precedent of Reb Yosef's answer and the precedent of Abraham's faith at the *Akeidah* are on entirely different levels than general legal precedents. Reb Yosef did not simply write down his answer, which the peasant was then able to understand, Reb Yosef actually brought down into the world the very potential for a person to create this idea in his own mind. A legal precedent transforms something which has always existed in potential to something which exists in the actual. Quite humbly, a scientist calls his own innovations "discoveries," as he is fully aware that they have been in effect well before his observation. Therefore to be the first in the legal and scientific world is entirely different to Abraham's first in the realm of self-sacrifice.

Abraham did not transform potential self-sacrifice into actual self-sacrifice, rather he "did the impossible," he brought down into the world a level of self-sacrifice that had never existed before.[10] Consequently,

---

10. This quality of self-sacrifice cannot be compared to the common conception of giving up one's life for a cause or simple suicide. Any person who dies for an ideal is not seeking to eliminate his ego, but rather to extend it. He basically believes that during his life he cannot have a sufficient impact upon the world, compared to the extent of which he will be remembered and admired if he were to give his life away. The classic suicide note begins with the words "Now you will have to take notice." The victim believes that the only way he can be heard is through the taking of his own life. In all such cases of so-called "self-sacrifice" the motive is not to eliminate one's ego and sphere of influence upon the world, but rather to increase it. Suicide, it is often said, is the ultimate act of selfishness,

all acts of self-sacrifice that came after the *Akeidah* required the relatively lesser effort of bringing the quality of self-sacrifice from the potential, which Abraham
had brought about, into the actual. Abraham "turned
on the tap" from which all future martyrs came to
drink.

TO SATURATE THE DAY

The *Akeidah* was not for publicity, as Abraham and
Isaac were alone, and it clearly contradicts the whole
purpose of Abraham's entire existence: to teach hu-
manity about God, since Isaac was the only successor
to this work, and his death would terminate a lifetime's
effort. The sole reason that Abraham was prepared to
sacrifice his son was simply that God willed it and
asked for it.

Through "opening the channel" of self-sacrifice,
Abraham elevated the *Akeidah* from an interesting and
historical event to a potent force in the everyday life
of a Jew. The *Akeidah* is not merely inspiring or enrich-
ing; by reading it in the morning prayers a person's
soul is actually affected, since these very same events
actually reoccur in microcosm within the reader.[11]

---

and if one understands that selfishness is the antithesis of
the belief in God, then clearly heroism and suicide have
absolutely no connection to *messiras nefesh*. The fundamental difference between giving up one's life for God and
giving it up for oneself is that the latter is a calculated and
rationalized activity, whereas true self-sacrifice is a totally
pure act that transcends all reasoning or goals.

11. *Shulchan Aruch Harav, Orach Chayim* (1st print)
(KPS, 1987), 1:10.

Opening the channel for self-sacrifice means that henceforth every single mitzvah performed by every single Jew is imbued and saturated with the same self-sacrifice as Abraham. When a Jew serves God, nobody has the right to criticize his motives, as all Jews share the spiritual legacy of their forefather, Abraham.[12]

THE SELF-SACRIFICE OF CHARITY

The Israeli Air Force was not terribly excited by the offer of a brand-new fighter jet costing $20,000,000. The funds were to be raised by a substantial contribution from each of the twenty wealthiest Jewish American philanthropists, who would collectively cover the entire cost of the plane. However, the head of the Israeli Air Force courteously refused the offer, explaining that "with twenty large plaques attached to the vehicle, it will have trouble leaving the ground."

Tzedakah is one of the easiest acts to criticize in terms of ulterior motives. So there is often an ambivalent reaction to the news that a large sum has been donated to charity. Most commonly there is a compromise of sentiments, that on the one hand the donation "will do a lot of good," but on the other hand the "large plaque" proudly proclaiming righteousness is somewhat incongruous. The true cynic cannot conceive that charity is anything more than a tranquilizer for the conscience.

However, every Jewish act of charity is perfectly defensible to even the greatest of cynics. The very notion that a Jew could do a mitzvah, particularly one so central as *tzedakah*, for purely selfish motivations is

---

12. *Hilchos Girushin* 2:20.

totally unthinkable, due to the influence of his soul. The effect of the Jewish soul upon one's deeds was totally transformed by Abraham at the *Akeidah*, and it was to an extent "reprogrammed" to function in the mode of self-sacrifice.

Subconsciously, every descendant of Abraham who has inherited the qualities of his soul wants to perform mitzvot in exactly the same manner as their Forefather who preceded them. Even if the person thinks that he is donating a sum of money purely for his own glory, this is merely an expression of how little he knows himself, rather than how selfish he actually is. The "reason," of course, is that his soul is part of a rare legacy from Abraham, which is predisposed to serve its Creator in a manner which transcends intellect. In a manner of true self-sacrifice, he is able to give *tzedakah* with all his might.

7

"The Sin of Sodom"— *Tzedakah* and the Non-Jew

In his book *The Sunflower*, Nazi hunter Simon Weisenthal describes an incident after the Holocaust in which a dying S.S. officer begged him for forgiveness for a catalogue of hideous crimes. The young Weisenthal simply refused this bizarre request, and left the Nazi's hospital room in silence. The purpose of *The Sunflower* was to relate this incident to twenty-four leading philosophers, and ask what they would do in the same situation.

Approximately half of the philosophers responded that they would have offered absolution, while the other half concurred with Weisenthal's conduct. However, the truly remarkable conclusion from this survey was that all of those who were prepared to forgive were Gentiles, while those who refused were all Jewish. Thus, in the realms of the intellectual secular philosopher, one of the most assimilated of environments, Jews and Gentiles proved to be different.

This truism has always been reflected in Jewish jurisprudence, where the obligations of a Gentile are totally different from those of a Jew. Unlike other religious legal systems, which offer "conversion or damnation," Jewish law recognizes and respects those who are "not of the faith," and has a wealth of laws and ethics to offer the non-Jew. Quantitatively and qualitatively, a Gentile has a different set of mitzvot than a Jew, and he has been "chosen" for an entirely different mission. Similarly, Chassidic philosophy emphasizes the uniqueness of each group, and stresses that each was created for a different purpose.[1]

It was therefore an extraordinary event when the Lubavitcher Rebbe announced on CNN in 1991 that a non-Jew has the ability to help bring the Messiah. The one mitzvah which the Rebbe singled out as the most important for a Gentile was the mitzvah of *tzedakah*. The Messiah will come "through increasing acts of goodness and kindness," He declared. With this unprecedented announcement, the Rebbe told the world that through giving *tzedakah* and acting in a "charitable" way, a Gentile could help fulfil the purpose of creation. However, such a unique declaration requires further analysis, since it is not even clear whether the giving of charity by a Gentile is actually a mitzvah— and thus a Divine legal obligation—or just an impressive moral action, possessing no Godly significance.

THE EXTREMES OF OMISSION

There is strong support from the Torah for the view that a Gentile is under a legal obligation to donate a portion of his wealth to charitable causes. The infa-

---

1. See *Likutei Sichos*, vol. 23, pp. 172–181.

mous city of Sodom was ultimately destroyed by God because its inhabitants did not give *tzedakah* to the needy: "This is the sin of Sodom . . . they did not strengthen the hand of the poor."[2] True, the inhabitants of Sodom are more renowned for the sins of idolatry, murder, and adultery; but the seemingly minor transgression of a failure to care sufficiently for the city's poor was actually the reason for the Divine destruction of the city, and for the consequent death of every inhabitant. Therefore, it was not merely hoped that Sodom would do the noble and altruistic act of charity, but it appears more accurate to state that they were under a legal duty to perform this as a Divine command. Despite the fact that they were not Jewish, the Sodomites were punished with the ultimate penalty of death and destruction for their failure to perform a mitzvah: the mitzvah for a Gentile to give *tzedakah*.

A lengthy discussion of the shortcomings of Sodom is found in the Talmud,[3] where it is recorded that the city of Sodom was incredibly fertile and its inhabitants were consequently men of great financial wealth. However, this "blessing of nature" was the cause of great selfishness and arrogance, and the prevailing attitude among the Sodomites was that "an abundance of bread grows from our earth, a bread which is made of gold: Why should we accept poor immigrants who will simply diminish our wealth?" Although Sodom was prepared to accept exceptionally rich immigrants such as Abraham's nephew, Lot, as a land of wealth and opportunity it had no interest in "your tired, and your poor, your huddled masses yearning to breathe

---

2. Ezek. 16:49.
3. *Sanhedrin* 109a.

free." Consequently, travelling through Sodom and immigrating into its boundaries was made illegal.[4]

THE MARTYRED GIRL

God told Abraham that He intended to destroy the Sodomites because "the outcry of Sodom has become great."[5] Many commentators interpret this to mean an "outcry" of defiance against God and his laws, and an arrogant, unacceptable rejection of His authority. However, the Ramban (R. Moshe ben Nachman, 1194–1270, in his classic *Commentary on the Torah*)

---

4. For those "fortunate" enough to enter the city, they would witness incredible cruelty, entirely sanctioned, and often imposed by the law courts of Sodom. The infamous courts of Sodom were headed by the Judges Shakrai, Shakurai, Zayafi, and Mazle Dina, whose judicial rulings included making a person who had been assaulted pay his assailant for the "opportunity to bleed." They also held that if a criminal chopped off the ear of a donkey, he would be awarded the donkey "until its ear grew back."

Guest houses for those who "holidayed" in Sodom were such that if a guest was too tall for his bed "they would chop off his feet," and if he were too small "they would stretch him" (Tractate *Sanhedrin* 109a). Clearly, one only went to Sodom once for a holiday! In fact, even when a poor man did manage to enter into Sodom, the Talmud relates that "each resident would give him a dinar, upon which he would write his name . . . so that when the poor man died, they could each reclaim their money." Such miserliness became progressively worse throughout the history of Sodom, and ultimately "feeding the starving and giving charity to the poor" became criminal offences (ibid.).

5. Gen. 18:20.

asserts that it was "an outcry of the oppressed, begging for help."

The Talmud teaches that Sodom was destroyed because of the "outcry of a [victimized] young girl."[6] This incident concerned a young girl bravely and charitably attempting to bring some bread to a very poor man. When the Sodomites heard of this breach of their criminal law against giving support to the poor, they "covered the girl in honey, placed her on a wall, and the bees came and consumed her."[7]

The fact that Sodom's destruction was based on the outcry of this young girl, due to her barbaric torture and eventual death, does not contradict the verse that states "this is the sin of Sodom"—the failure to give *tzedakah*. The Sodomites did not only murder an innocent young girl, they also killed a helper of the poor. They illustrated utter contempt for the laws of *tzedakah*, by their torture and killing of one who courageously sought to perform the mitzvah. The omission of charity among the Sodomites was so extreme that an extreme penalty was deemed necessary—ultimate destruction and annihilation. Clearly, a Gentile is obligated to give *tzedakah* in Jewish law.

Yet, as a descendant of Noah, every non-Jew is obligated only for seven laws.[8] The seven mitzvahs which were given to Noah and which are legal obligations upon every Gentile today are laws relating to: (1)

---

6. *Sanhedrin* 109a.

7. The view of the Ramban as to the plain meaning of the verse is consistent with the Talmud's homiletical interpretation that the outcry was "great" (in the Hebrew verse, the word "Rabbah"), however the Talmud states that the "outcry was not Rabbah (great), but Ribbah" (meaning due to "the young girl").

8. Rambam, *Mishneh Torah, Hilchos Melachim*, ch. 9–10.

idolatry, (2) murder, (3) theft, (4) blasphemy, (5) sexual morality, (6) establishing a legal system, and (7) not eating a limb torn from a living animal.

The obligation to give charity is not listed amongst these seven, and since these are the only mitzvot which a Gentile is legally required to do, it does not appear to be an "obligatory mitzvah" for a non-Jew to give *tzedakah*. If this is the case, why did the entire city of Sodom deserve to be destroyed?

A HOUSEHOLD OF HUMANITARIANS

God said of Abraham, "I have loved him because he has commanded his children and his household after him, that they keep My ways, doing justice and *tzedakah*."[9] This praise is not only the explanation for God's decision to warn Abraham of His plan to destroy Sodom, but it is also the rationale for the very destruction itself.

The men and women in Abraham's household (and by extension, all non-Jews) were given the commandment "to do justice and *tzedakah*."[10] Therefore, God's love for Abraham, and the reason He told him of His plan to destroy Sodom, was on the basis that Abraham had elevated the giving of *tzedakah* to the level of a mitzvah. *Tzedakah* was now, thanks to Abraham, awarded the status of a "Noachide law."[11]

---

9. Gen. 18:19.

10. Although some commentators assert that the word *tzedakah* in this context means righteousness (and others even argue that it means "to teach compromise"—Rashi), the Yad Rama confidently asserts that it means literal *tzedakah*—the giving of charity to the poor.

11. *Sanhedrin* 57b.

However, if *tzedakah* became a legal obligation for every Gentile subsequent to Abraham's command, if it became a Noachide law, why is it not among the seven famous obligations?

A solution is to be found in the very nature of the seven laws themselves. The seven Noachide laws are all of the category of *Shev V'al Taase* ("sit and don't do"). Legally, they are all prohibitions; thus one is commanded to "sit and don't do them." However, *tzedakah* comes under the category of a *Koom V'aase* ("stand up and do"). Therefore, *tzedakah* does not fit among the seven Noachide laws because it is an obligation of commission, while the seven are obligations of omission.[12] *Tzedakah* is thus a basic legal obligation upon every individual, and the fact that it is not explicit within the seven Noachide laws seems to be a mere technicality. The Ran (R. Nissim of Gerona, 1290–1375) concludes that it is for this technical reason that *tzedakah* is excluded from the list of seven, and its omission does not negate its power as a positive obligation upon every human being.

However, in his *Mishneh Torah* (fourteen volumes, covering every aspect of Jewish law), the Rambam appears to disagree. He asserts that *Bnei Noach* (Gentiles) are not legally obligated to give *tzedakah*. This ruling can be implied from the words of the Rambam,

---

12. Tractate *Sanhedrin* (58b) discusses the fact that the obligation to establish Courts of Law (one of the Seven) appears to be a "*Koom V'aase*" (mitzvah of commission). However, the Talmud concludes that the law is basically that one *omit* to pervert the course of justice. It is thus a law of commission and omission, and the average *Bnei Noach* who is unable to set up a legal system is expected to keep the "sit and don't do" aspect of not disrupting justice.

when he holds that if a Gentile "wishes to perform
extra good deeds . . . which he is not obligated to do,
in order to receive a reward . . . [one among the many
is that] he should give *tzedakah*."[13] This appears to be
a conclusive legal ruling that for a Gentile, giving charity is desirable and meritorious, rather than obligatory.

Unfortunately, an irreconcilable difficulty seems
to have arisen, to the extent that if *tzedakah* is one of
the mitzvot of *Bnei Noach*, there should be eight mitzvahs, rather that seven. While if one is to conclude (as
the Rambam) that *tzedakah* is not a mitzvah for *Bnei
Noach*, we cannot justify the total destruction of Sodom.

RAMBAM VERSUS RAMBAN

It is common in Jewish scholarship for a multitude of
intellectual difficulties to be reconciled by a simple
stroke of genius. Frequently, it is a case of the Ramban
"to the rescue," as his erudition and deep understanding of the Torah have proven capable of anticipating
questions which would be asked centuries later.

In his analysis of the legal obligations of a Gentile,
the Ramban clearly answers the two principal questions as to why *tzedakah* does not appear among the
"seven" explicit obligations of non-Jews, and also why
Sodom deserved to be destroyed. The sixth Noachide
mitzvah, which is to "establish a legal system," is not
solely an obligation to set up courts and appoint judges.
This legal obligation involves all matters of ensuring
law and justice, such as establishing appropriate laws
concerning civil matters, to ensure equitable business
regulation, having an acceptable political system, and

13. *Mishneh Torah, Laws of Kings*, 10:10.

encouraging general morality. Therefore, the Ramban holds that the sixth Noachide law, the obligation to establish a legal system, also includes the mitzvah of *tzedakah*. *Tzedakah* is not "one of the seven," it is a part of one of the seven obligations.[14]

However, the Rambam once again disagrees. According to his investigation of the Noachide laws,[15] the sixth mitzvah of establishing a legal system only includes the strict legal obligation of appointing judges and setting up courts of law specifically to enforce the other six Noachide laws. According to the Rambam's understanding of Jewish law, the mitzvah of *tzedakah* is not a specific legal obligation for a Gentile. Consequently, the destruction of Sodom once more appears a little unfair.

THE "SEVEN" IN JEWISH JURISPRUDENCE

The fundamental basis of the Jewish Legal system is that God instituted 613 laws with which a Jew can refine the world. Jewish law exists for the purpose of making the world an "inhabitable residence" for the Almighty, and the means by which this is achieved is learning Torah and performing mitzvahs. Hence, Jew-

---

14. Even though the Ramban accepts that the death sentence is only appropriate for those who transgress the negative prohibitions—and *tzedakah* is a positive command, an act of commission—this only applies to a human court. Thus, Sodom's failure to give *tzedakah* may not merit the death penalty down here, but it does deserve a Divine punishment. The Sodomites merited and received death "by the Hand of Heaven."

15. *Laws of Kings* 9:14.

ish law is not merely intended for the purposes of a
harmonious society, or enforced for the sake of general morality. The jurisprudential basis of Jewish law
is that it is simply the Divine Will: God wants certain
things to be done. When a Jew fulfils these obligations
and refrains from breaches of Jewish law, he is fulfilling the ultimate purpose of creation, to refine the
world to the satisfaction of its Creator.[16]

In contrast, the seven Noachide laws are for the
purpose of creating a peaceful and harmonious world.
This engenders the appropriate atmosphere in which
a Jew can perform his 613 obligations. The laws of a
Gentile are thus not an end in themselves, they are a
means toward higher ends. Therefore the Jew and the
Gentile exist in a form of partnership: the Jew requires
the Gentile to keep his seven laws in order to facilitate
a Jew's performance of mitzvot. Simultaneously, a
Gentile requires a Jew to keep his 613, in order that the
purpose of creation be fulfilled.[17]

---

16. Rashi explains that the first word of the Torah,
"*Bereishis*," is not only understood as "In the Beginning
[God created the world]," but can also be translated as
"*B-Reishis*," meaning "For two reasons [God created the
world]." These "two reasons," asserts Rashi, are "the Jews
and the Torah." Consequently, the 613 laws that a Jew must
fulfill are not means toward some greater end, but are the
very reason for which the world was created.

17. However, see *Likutei Sichos*, vol. 23, p. 179, where
the Rebbe articulates a revolutionary stance (based upon
the Rambam) that non-Jews will enjoy personal reward
in the final and complete redemption not as a consequence
of helping Jews, but as a direct effect of performing their
own mitzvahs.

Although the seven commandments of a Gentile may appear inferior, and merely "democratic" in nature, from a jurisprudential perspective, they are as "Theocratic" as the laws of a Jew. God explicitly commanded the Gentile to perform seven mitzvahs, the observance of which are vital in the Divine plan. So even according to the Rambam's analysis that the mitzvah of *tzedakah* is not one of the seven Noachide laws, it is still arguable that the "sin" of Sodom was the equivalent of a breach of all seven. The failure of the Sodomites to "strengthen the hand of the poor" contradicted the very purpose of the seven Noachide laws, since a "peaceful and harmonious society" in which a Jew can perform his mitzvahs, clearly demands a "moral" and "charitable" disposition on the part of the Gentile populace.[18]

It was not necessarily the breach of a specific Noachide law that necessitated the punishment of the Sodomites; the Rambam would argue that it was the "outcry of Sodom," the exceptional way in which they failed to give *tzedakah*, which necessitated their destruction.[19] An extreme failure to give *tzedakah* appears to be a fundamental breach of the whole purpose of the seven Noachide laws. Conversely, the act of giving *tzedakah*, "performing acts of goodness and

---

18. *Likutei Sichos*, vol. 5, p. 159.

19. The miserliness of Sodom was so extreme they did not merely omit to give *tzedakah*, they actually made the giving of *tzedakah* a criminal offence. The extremity of their omission to give, and the perversion of their own legal system, extended to the torture and murder of those who chose to give *tzedakah*, and it is also for these reasons that Sodom was held to be "sinful."

kindness," is a "positive" way in which a Gentile is able to fulfill the spirit and very purpose of all his seven obligations.[20]

Although the laws of a Gentile are all negative prohibitions, a list of seven things which a Gentile must not do, the Lubavitcher Rebbe in his advice on CNN appears to have summarized the seven Noachide laws for the world in one positive message: "Acts of goodness and kindness" are the means by which a Gentile facilitates a Jew's performance of mitzvahs; and so that which a non-Jew achieves by means of keeping all his negative precepts he can also accomplish with the "positive mitzvah" of *tzedakah.*

---

20. Furthermore, in 1991 the Rebbe initiated a campaign to publicize the mitzvah of *tzedakah* to non-Jews in particular. See *Sefer HaSichos* 5752, vol. 2, p. 372, n. 94, where the Rebbe refers to the arguments articulated in this chapter as the legal basis for this campaign.

In that essay, the Rebbe explains why the performance of mitzvahs by non-Jews, particularly the mitzvah of *tzedakah,* is intrinsically linked with the imminence of redemption, since it signifies that the human mind has itself come to recognize the truth of Torah, rather than it being enforced from "above." Hence, this is commensurate with the theme of redemption, where the earth itself becomes filled with the knowledge of God (Isa. 11:9). (See also *Moses of Oxford* [Andre Deutsch, 1994, p. 479], where Rabbi Shmuel Boteach uses this argument as a defense for inviting Mikhail Gorbachev, a secular peacemaker, to speak for a religious society.)

8

To Be *and* Not To Be

The tenuous nature of reality is described by Reb Azrielke of Miropolye, the "Great" Chassidic Rebbe in Shlomo Ansky's Yiddish play *The Dybbuk*. In a sublime Chassidic discourse which acts as the play's foundation, Reb Azrielke inspires his listeners with the following oration:

"God's world is holy and great. The holiest land in the world is Israel. The holiest city in Israel is Jerusalem. The holiest place in Jerusalem was the Temple, and the holiest spot in the Temple was the Holy of Holies.

"There are seventy nations in the world, and among them the people of Israel is the holiest. And the tribe of Levi is the holiest of the twelve tribes of Israel, and among the Levites the holiest are the priests. And among the priests the holiest is the High Priest.

"There are 354 days in the year, and among them the holy days are sacred. And the Sabbath is holier than the holy days. And the holiest of all the holy days, the

93

Sabbath of Sabbaths, is Yom Kippur, which is the Day of Atonement.

"There are seventy languages in the world, and the holiest among them is Hebrew. And the holiest work in the Hebrew language is the Torah, and its holiest part is the Ten Commandments, and the holiest word in the Ten Commandments is the name of God.

"Once a year, on Yom Kippur, the four holiest sanctities gather together precisely when the High Priest enters the Holy of Holies in order to pronounce the ineffable name of God. And at this immeasurably holy and awesome moment the High Priest and the people of Israel are in the utmost peril, for even a single sinful or wayward thought in the High Priest's mind at that instant might, God forbid, destroy the entire world.

"Every piece of ground on which a person stands when he raises his eyes to heaven is a Holy of Holies; everyone created in the image of God is a High Priest; every day in a person's life is Yom Kippur, and every word which a person speaks from his heart is God's name. Therefore, every sin and every wrong committed by man brings the world to destruction."[1]

Such an approach would appear to *guarantee* the annihilation of the world for sins such as the "golden calf." However, atonement for even this sin was awarded to the Jewish people by means of their giving the "half-shekel" to the Sanctuary. The "multi-purpose" mitzvah of *shekalim*, which the Talmud deems to have been substituted in the modern era by the mitzvah of *tzedakah*, can boast profound powers of salvation. Not only did this form of charity save the Jews from de-

---

1. Based on *Mishnah Keilim* 1:6–9.

struction during their "calf-worshipping desert wandering days," it also came to their rescue more than 1,000 years later, during the story of Purim.

A PERFECT EXCHANGE RATE

In the Talmud, Raish Lakish states that God knew at the time of creation that "In the future, Haman would offer *shekalim* [to the King of Persia, in order to destroy] the Jewish people. Therefore God pre-empted Haman's shekels with those of the Jews."[2] This meant that the collective merit of all the *shekalim* donated to charity by the Jews would prove sufficient to outweigh the financial offer which Haman would make to the King as an inducement to destroy them. The inevitable result would be the *tzedakah* of the Jews "at war" with the money of Haman.

Since God is omniscient, and knows that which will happen in the future, He made a pre-emptive bid to protect His chosen people, by making sure that they gave large amounts of money to *tzedakah*: this ensured that when the decree of Haman arose, the Jews would have sufficient "credit" to outweigh the forces of evil.

The Iyun Yaakov comments that Haman's intention was that the large sum of money which he contributed to the King (as an inspiration for the annihilation of the Jews) should be stored and distributed for charity. Therefore, Haman's plan had great strength behind it, since it was supported by an enormous donation to *tzedakah* of 10,000 *kikkars* of silver (approximately $100,000,000 at the current price of silver). This

---

2. *Meggilah* 13b, Jerusalem Talmud 1:5.

tactical move was anticipated by God, and was the
basis of His instituting the mitzvah of the half a shekel.
Hence, God's pre-emptive move was not really an indis-
criminate "mitzvah-attack" upon Haman, but rather
a calculated plan, whereby the Jews giving *tzedakah*
would counteract Haman's charitable donation.

A further illustration of God's foresight and attention to detail is provided by a comment of Tosafos, "That
I have heard [an explanation] that the 10,000 silver
kikkars of Haman are the exact total of one half-shekel
for every one of the 600,000 Jews who left Egypt."
Tosafos concludes by stating, "Check these calculations
and you will find that the figures are exact." This high-
lights the fact that not only was the mitzvah of the half-
a-shekel a merit for the Jews and a direct counterbalance for Haman's contribution, but the sum total of
all the Jew's half shekels was to equal precisely Haman's
bribe to the King of 10,000 *kikkars*.

The Bach notes that the half-shekel was a mitzvah
incumbent upon every male from the age of twenty
until seventy. Hence, the lifetime contribution per Jew
was twenty-five shekels (fifty years × half-shekel). Thus,
600,000 Jews contributed 15,000,000 shekels, and since
one *kikkar* of silver has an exchange rate of 1,500 shekels, the Jews collectively donated 10,000 *kikkars*. The
entire Jewish people fulfilled the mitzvah of *shekalim*
to the worth of $100,000,000 of silver. One thousand
years later, Haman offered an identical sum for their
destruction.

In this light, the words of the Talmud, "He pre-
empted Haman's shekels with those of the Jews" takes
on new significance. Almost 1,000 years before the
events of Purim, a new mitzvah of giving half a shekel
annually was introduced. By careful planning, the
collective value of all the Jews, based upon their lifetime contribution to *tzedakah*, was to equal exactly the

"bribe of *tzedakah*" which Haman was to offer the King in exchange for signing a decree against the Jews. God's foresight was engineered with ultimate precision.

A *"TOICHENDICKER FAARBUND"*

The Baal Shem-Tov, the founder of the Chassidic movement (1698–1760), explained that the necessity to find the contemporary relevance of every aspect of the Torah is a direct command from the Oral Law.[3] The Mishnah states that "any person who reads the megillah backwards, is not considered to have fulfilled his obligation" to read this text on Purim.[4] The Baal Shem-Tov suggests that this law seems to be of little practical relevance, since the very suggestion is preposterous.[5] Therefore, he interprets "backwards-reading" not as reading the words in the reverse order, but rather perceiving the text as having only an historical significance. Therefore, if a person reads the megillah and finds it merely "interesting," he has not fulfilled his obligation until he finds it instructive.[6] This creates a

---

3. Quoted in *"Divrei Shalom," Parshas Bo.* See *Likutei Sichos*, vol. 6, 3rd ed. (KPS, 1990), pp. 189, 385.

4. *Megillah* 17a.

5. However, this law is brought in *Shulchan Aruch* (*Orach Chayim* 590:6, and *Taz*, ibid).

6. It is well-known that the etymological root of the word Torah is *"Hohrah,"* meaning "directive" (see *Zohar*, vol. 3, 53b, and also *Hadranim al HaRambam veShas* (KPS, 1992), p. 47, n. 19). This attests to the fact that every single detail mentioned within the written or oral Torah contains within it a universal lesson and message for all generations. Hence, if a person were to learn a portion of the Torah, and

difficulty with the Talmudic discussion concerning "Haman's shekels," which seems entirely historical in nature and of no direct contemporary significance.

One point that does stand out is the omniscience of God. It would therefore seem that the Talmud is teaching the profound lesson of God's particular supervision in every aspect of the world, and His intense love for the Jewish people. Nevertheless, this is a lesson which could be learned from a variety of other places throughout the Torah, and does not necessitate the mentioning of this particular incident.

That which really requires understanding is the precise directive of this particular piece of Talmud, which distinguishes it from all other parts of the Oral Law. A good interpretation must make full use of every detail related in the Talmud, and illustrate how it relates to the specific directive. In Yiddish, this is affectionately known as a *"Toichendiker faarbund,"* meaning an intrinsic and all-encompassing connection. Clearly, in a Talmudic passage that deals with subjects of such great variety as (1) Haman, (2) a decree against the Jewish people, and (3) silver coins to *tzedakah*, there must be a profound explanation which shows precisely what all these details mean in a practical sense, and the thread that ties them together.

---

derive only information of historical interest or miscellaneous facts, this conclusion itself would indicate that the entire message of the Torah has been lost. Furthermore, it is not the style of the Torah to present unnecessary details, and thus if a person's understanding of a certain part of the Torah does not explain the necessity for all the details involved, it can be assured that the true interpretation has not been found.

TO EXIST AND TO KNOW

The "charity-war" between the Jews and Haman can be fully appreciated through a thorough understanding of the Existence of God, as described in Jewish sources. The Rambam states at the beginning of his magnum opus, the *Mishneh Torah* (in which he codifies the entire Torah), that it is a mitzvah—I. *"TO KNOW THAT THERE IS A FIRST BEING, AND THAT HE BROUGHT EVERYTHING INTO EXISTENCE."*[7]

The Rambam continues with the same theme in his second Law—II. *"AND IF IT ARISES IN [YOUR] KNOWL-*

---

7. It is self-evident that in expressing such a profound principle of the Jewish faith, the Rambam was extremely precise in the choice of words with which he chose to express this law. On this basis, a number of points require explanation: (a) Why did the Rambam choose the expression "Being," but fail to explain what type of "being" he refers to? In fact, the mitzvah is to believe that there is a God, which does not seem well described by merely stating "being," a word which can be used to refer to any simple creation. (b) Since the Rambam uses the words "that He brings everything into existence," the additional emphasis that God is "first," seems totally superfluous. Surely, if a person has come to the realization that God created the "everything in existence," it is quite obvious that He is "first." (c) Furthermore, the term "first" also has derogatory connotations, since it implies that the described entity is the "first" of a number of similar entities. In other words, objects are only counted if they possess some common theme. Therefore, it appears somewhat insulting to state that God is "first," since it implies that He has some similarity with His creations, which is clearly untrue.

EDGE THAT HE IS NON-EXISTENT, THEN NOTHING ELSE COULD POSSIBLY EXIST."[8]

While the precise wording of the Rambam is somewhat strange and raises many intellectual difficulties, all problems are resolved by an innovatory speech of the Lubavitcher Rebbe on these two laws.[9]

The Rebbe explains that in order to be accessible to His creations, God "belittled" Himself[10] so as to exist in a state which can be described by the word "Being." So, while in essence God totally transcends any comprehension, nevertheless He Himself chose to "create" an appearance to which His creations could relate. It was only after assuming this form, that God created the world.

It is for this reason that the Rambam used the term "First Being" in reference to the creation of the world, since the aspect of God which created the world is al-

---

8. Similarly, there are a number of difficulties with this second law: (a) What new information in being presented in this Law? Surely, after a person has already learned in the first law that "everything that exists . . . only exists from the truth of His existence," it is quite obvious that everything depends upon God. (b) What was the Rambam's intent when writing the lengthy expression, "And if it arises in [Your] knowledge," when the word "if" would appear to suffice: the law could simply state, "If God didn't exist, then nothing else could exist"? (c) The phrase, "He is non-existent," is confusing, and seems self-contradictory, since "He is" implies existence, but "non-existence" clearly negates this.

9. The Rebbe, *Hadranim al HaRambam veShas* (KPS, 5745), pp. 39–77.

10. Naturally, in His "essence," God remained unaffected by this.

ready after the process of "belittlement." Hence, it is appropriate to use the words "First" and "Being" which imply that God is somewhat compatible to the world. The Rambam does not use the word "God" in his first law (since "God" implies "transcendence"), but rather teaches that there is a mitzvah to know that God is "First Being," that He exists within the world, and is "immanent."[11]

In contrast, the second law of the Rambam discusses the aspect of God that does totally transcends the world. Therefore the term "non-existence" is employed, as from such a lofty perspective of God the word "existence" could not possibly apply. Furthermore, in order to ensure that this statement would be understood in this sense, and not as a question of whether or not God exists, the Rambam stated clearly the words "He is non-existent." In this context, the word "He" negates any possibility of learning erroneously that God does not exist whatsoever, since "He" clearly refers to the one that "brought everything into existence" (mentioned in the first law). The innovation of this second law is that, in addition to the fact that He is found immanent in the world, God also transcends the world.

---

11. This theme is expressed in the Talmudic dictum that "In the place of His greatness, there you will find His humility" (Tractate *Meggilah* 31a). In this statement, "the place of His greatness" means "the World" (see Tractate *Berachos* 58a), and the message being expressed is simply that the greatest imaginable acts of God are pitiful in comparison to His true abilities. Therefore, that which we perceive as greatness is for God a tremendous act of humility. In common terms, the oft-spoken infinitude and omniscience of God represent His "accessibility," rather than His essence.

This, also sheds light on the Rambam's strange expression "if it arises in [your] knowledge." Since the aspect of God that is totally beyond creation represents a more sophisticated and lofty conception of Him, the Rambam emphasizes this intellectual leap by stating that this is an ascent in knowledge ("arises in your knowledge").

. . . AND NOT TO BE.

The first two laws of the *Mishneh Torah* are therefore stating the two most significant facts that a Jew has to know about his Creator: firstly, that God is a "First Being" to the extent that He exists within the world, and is totally compatible and accessible to His creations; secondly, if a person were to attempt a more sophisticated approach and try to appreciate the aspect of God that is "non-existent"—to the point of being beyond the world and human comprehension—he must not make the mistake of thinking that this is all God has to offer.[12] If this were true, if God only transcended the world, but had no connection with it, then the Rambam asserts that "nothing else could possibly exist."

Ultimately both aspects of God exist together: He is found in the world, and at the same time, transcends it. In effect, a Jew has an obligation to know two facts: first, that God is immanent in the world, he exists in the manner of "to be." In addition to this, a Jew must also know that God remains aloof from any definition

---

12. This is the mistake of Spinoza, whose philosophy of Deism denies the existence of a personal God who communicates with human beings.

that we could assign to Him, and so it can be stated that He is also "not to be." In effect, God is "to be" and "not to be" all at once.

A GAPING HOLE TO FILL

Haman's plan to exterminate the Jews was not only by means of the *tzedakah* which he gave, but it also centered around the casting of a "lot," to determine the date of the proposed destruction. (This is not merely an incidental detail, since the entire festival of Purim is named after this device: *"Pur"* is Persian for a "lot.") While the use of a lot may appear trivial, Chassidic philosophy explains that it was the cause for the incredible potency of Haman's plan.

Essentially, a lot is a device which rejects the priorities of the world. When an individual casts a lot, he is effectively rejecting all the intellectual arguments and emotional drives which render one of his own choices more compelling. Chassidic philosophy explains that by discarding all matters of sense and desire which exist within the world and choosing to rely upon a simple lottery, a person succeeds in leaving an "open channel" for higher forms of inspiration.[13] Haman recognized that there are levels of Godliness that transcend the world and he desired to harness the power of these levels of Godliness for his own evil purposes. Through casting the lot and giving vast sums to *tzedakah*, he hoped to access the transcendent aspects of God, on the assumption that if the world is insignificant to God at this level, then so are His chosen people, the Jews.

---

13. *Sefer Maamorim* 5713 (KPS, 1988), pp. 376–378.

However, 1,000 years earlier, God had anticipated Haman's attempt to access the transcendent realm for the purposes of destruction, and therefore God armed the Jews with the mitzvah of *shekalim*, which would prove sufficient to counteract Haman's plan. Hence, it was through the unique mitzvah of the *tzedakah* of the half-shekel that the Jews were able to be victorious over an adversary who was drawing on the power of a lot—a strength from beyond this world. God granted them this power in advance since He saw that in the future the Jews would be in a situation of dire need, with their very lives in danger.

"OUT OF THIS WORLD DONATIONS"

The classic reason for which God gave the Jews the mitzvah to give half a shekel, was to fulfil the function of atonement (principally for the sin of the golden calf). The route by which atonement is achieved must also transcend the world, because a sin takes place within the world. So thus, in order to achieve forgiveness from God, the Jew must appeal to God as He transcends the world. At this level the world, its problems, and its sins are insignificant.

To reach so high, the Jew must restrengthen his relationship with the Divine by emphasizing that God is more important to him than anything the world has to offer. Any energy for the Jews to achieve this task of atonement was granted through the mitzvah of the half a shekel (see chapter 1, above).

This explains why the Talmud speaks specifically of (1) Haman's plan and (2) its nullification by the mitzvah of *shekalim*. Both of these two incidents stand out in the respect that they represent the accessing of Godliness as it transcends the world. The Jewish mitzvah of the *shekalim* had the power to destroy the decree of Haman, since it also drew on a strength that is "out of this world." God anticipated a future need for this great power and so granted it to the Jews, 1,000 years in advance.[14]

Although *shekalim* can no longer be given, the Talmud explains that the concept has a practical significance today, since it represents an increase in the mitzvah of *tzedakah*. "When the Temple stood, a person would bring his shekel and thereby achieve atonement. Now that the Temple no longer stands . . . *tzedakah* is a good [substitute]."[15]

Such unique achievements are reflected in a profound similarity between the mitzvah of *tzedakah* and *shekalim*, since they are both mitzvot which are performed "in response to a need." *Shekalim* was instituted in response to a need to nullify the decree of Haman, and the mitzvah of *tzedakah* clearly represents responding to a need which a poor person has. This similarity is an important indication of the common power that these two mitzvahs possess.

The Talmud explains that due to a "future" time of great national emergency, the mitzvah of *shekalim* was innovated. It was endowed with a unique power to reach the transcendent realm, and as its "modern-day counterpart" the mitzvah of *tzedakah* can boast the same.

---

14. See *Sefer Sichos* 5751 (KPS, 1992), vol. 1, pp. 323–324.

15. *Bava Basra* 9a.

9

A Diamond
under Duress

A famous story concerns the Greek philosopher Aristotle, who was considered the very pillar of morality in ancient times. The entire world was well-versed in his works, which were acclaimed as the classic statement of how a human being should behave. So one can imagine the surprise of Aristotle's students upon discovering a rumor that their master had visited a dubious part of town. In total disbelief, they rushed straight to the alleged house of ill-repute to dispel the vicious gossip which had spread throughout Athens.

On arriving at their destination, shock and despair rapidly spread among Aristotle's students, as it was revealed to their own eyes that the rumors were in fact true. They begged for an explanation: "How could the great Aristotle be found in such a lowly place?"

"When I am in the lecture theatre," replied the philosopher, "then I am Aristotle. Now, in this place, I am not Aristotle."

GIVING NOTHING AT ALL

"To practice what you preach" may not have been an important value in Greek society, but within Jewish philosophy it has always been the top priority. Therefore, in quantitative terms, the amount of written Jewish works that are devoted exclusively to morals is somewhat minimal, since values are principally transmitted and learned through personal contact with one's teachers. Nevertheless, the very essence of Jewish ethics has been encapsulated in a major work, known as the *Ethics of the Fathers*.[1]

In the fifth chapter of this monumental work, there is a list of "the four attitudes among those who give charity": (1) "One who wishes to give, but that others should not—he begrudges others." (2) "One who wishes others should give, and he should not—he begrudges himself." (3) "One who wishes to give, and that others should too—he is a Chassid (pious)." (4) "One who wishes not to give, and that others should not give also—he is wicked."[2]

However, there seems to be a logical flaw in this list, since by definition it is supposed to describe only those "who give charity." Why are we introduced to "four types of givers" when only three members of the list are willing to give at all? The fourth individual "who wishes not to give, and that others should not give also" is in absolutely no way a "giver" of charity,

---

1. The Hebrew name for the Mishnah *Ethics of the Fathers* is simply *Avos*, meaning "Fathers," and thus the emphasis is placed upon the individual sages who personified these ethics, rather than the abstract moral ideal.
2. *Avos* 5:13.

neither by himself or through others.[3] Why is a man who is "wicked" and "fails to give" included in a list of those who are labelled "charitable"?[4]

COUNTING DIAMONDS

Every Sunday morning for several years, the Lubavitcher Rebbe (Rabbi Menachem Mendel Schneersohn) would distribute dollar bills to be donated to charity. People would wait for hours in a seemingly endless line, along Eastern Parkway, Brooklyn, for a dollar and a blessing from the Rebbe, which would last for only a few seconds. It was always a point of discus-

---

3. R. Ovadiah Bertinoro (1445–1505) explains that we are discussing the four types of "giving" *tzedakah*, rather than the "givers." However, this does not fit well, according to the simple meaning of the text.

4. While the second individual's failure to give may be inexcusable, his wish that others should donate is of great importance, particularly if he actively encourages such benevolence. In fact, the Talmud (*Bava Basra* 9a) states that "the encouraging/inspiring of others to give, is even greater than to give by oneself." This is based upon the philosophy espoused in Isaiah (32:17) and explained by the Ritva (R. Yom Tov Ibn Ashvili, 1260–1328). With gratitude to the erudition, profound scholarship, and devotion to detail of HaRav Moshe Yehudah HaKohen Blau Shlita, the Ritva's commentary on *Bava Basra* became available in 1951. This work explains the greatness of inspiring another to give *tzedakah* by asserting that the "calm and security" which a gift to *tzedakah* achieves is merely of "temporary benefit." However, the encouraging of a gift by another achieves "Peace," which is a "complete and permanent good."

sion among the week's visitors as to how remarkable was the sheer physical stamina of a man in his late eighties who would stand for five hours or more, without a break or the slightest lapse in attention.

One particular woman on reaching the front of the line could not help but express her immense wonderment at the Rebbe's strength and patience, and exclaimed, "I am much younger than you, and standing here I have become exhausted. How is it that you don't ever become tired with so many people coming to visit you?"

The Rebbe smiled and replied, "When you are counting diamonds, you don't get tired."

To a person who truly appreciates and loves a Jew, he sees only a diamond. True, it may be a "slightly soiled" diamond, but it is nevertheless of incredible value and can easily be cleaned. If a Jew does not presently wish to give to charity, this does not mean that he is not a "giver" of *tzedakah*, but simply his genuine will has been temporarily concealed by a "little bit of dirt"—intrinsically, he really wants to give.

Therefore, the reason why a "non-giver" is included in a list which is only for "givers" is due to the fact that his lack of enthusiasm to give is more of a "bad mood" than his genuine disposition. Chassidic thought says that for a Jew, evil is an abnormality, a "superficial infection" which can be removed quickly and without a trace. The Jewish soul is like a diamond, and its brightness shines from every facet. As a diamond, it is "harder" than all of its surroundings and so cannot be affected by them.

Consequently, the list of four givers is in fact presenting a profound innovation. Stating that even a person who is on such a level that he actually "does not give and does not want others to give," is nevertheless included amongst the "givers," since his true and inner will is, in the words of the Rambam, "to be a Jew . . . [and] to perform all the mitzvahs."[5]

While the suggestion that a Jew is fundamentally righteous may at first glance appear difficult to accept, a close analysis of the texts reveals that this is not a case of Chassidic optimism, but is rather a basic principle in Jewish law.

THE EVIL INCLINATION: INCITING THE BAD

In the Rambam's *Mishneh Torah*,[6] a case is quoted where a Jewish court (*Beis Din*) has demanded a man grant his wife's request for a divorce, and yet he refuses to do so. In such a situation, Jewish law recommends that any method at the court's disposal can be employed to encourage the man to consent to the wife's request. Even physical violence applied by the court is an acceptable and lawful procedure and the Rambam states that the court may "beat him until he says 'I consent.'" The reason which justifies this seemingly drastic measure is that since the husband is a Jew "he desires . . . to perform all the mitzvahs and avoid any transgression," and since the demand of the court is based upon the Torah, it is assumed that he genuinely wishes to consent to it. The only reason for his reluctance must be because "his evil inclination incited him, and thus he is beaten until his evil inclination is weakened and he offers his consent—[and thus it is considered as if] he granted the divorce voluntarily."

---

5. See *Sefer Hisvadiyus* 5747, vol. 4 (Kfar Chabad: Lahak Hanochos, 1949), pp. 221–225.

6. *Hilchos Girushin* (Laws of Divorce 2:20).

It may initially be difficult to accept the validity of a legal authority which sanctions violence as a means to achieve its goals. Although many legal systems employ some form of corporal or capital punishment for those who transgress the law, here the "beating" of the unobliging husband is not for the sake of punishment. The Jewish court does not sanction violence on the grounds that the husband is a criminal, but rather because he is a victim: a victim of his evil inclination. The "beating" is not intended as a deterrent to others or a punishment for him, it is simply an assault upon his evil inclination, which is "inciting" him to transgress the mitzvah of following the court's ruling to give his wife a divorce. Since Jewish law assumes that a Jew's inner will is to perform all mitzvahs, the husband is separated from his "evil inciter" by means of the beating, and is then in the position of performing his true inner will, to perform the mitzvah without any interference.

A WITNESS FOR THE PROSECUTION

A melodramatic American lawyer would conclude each of his closing speeches for the defense in the same manner: he would build up to a profound crescendo, having silenced the audience and brought the jury close to tears with a moving rendition of the difficulties which his client had endured throughout his life. The lawyer would then place his hands into his briefcase, pull out his closed fists, and slowly walk toward the jury.

"Ladies and Gentlemen of the jury," the lawyer would begin, "in my hands I have a small, defenseless bird, of whom I ask each of you the question: Is this bird alive or is it dead? However, this is a question which you are totally unable to predict correctly; as either way, I could ensure your failure. If you guess that this bird is dead, I will simply open my hands, and it will immediately fly to safety. Yet, if you guess that the small bird is alive, I need only tighten my grip, and consequently when I open my hands, the bird will be dead."

The Lawyer would then point toward his client, and conclude that "the same as the fate of this small bird in my hands, so too is the life of this defendant: totally *in your hands*."

Since the Rambam rules that life and death and good and evil are totally *in the hands* of every individual,[7] a Jew can be punished for his sins, even though he was incited by his evil inclination to perform them. The Rambam did not write that the evil inclination places a Jew under duress; he simply described it as an inciter not to give, so that a claim that "I inherently wish to give to *tzedakah*, and only become a 'non-giver' due to the incitement of my evil inclination" is no defense in Jewish law. Any individual has a valid legal defense if he has committed a crime under duress.[8]

---

7. *Hilchos Teshuvah* (Laws of Repentance 5:1–4) explains that "Free will is bestowed upon every human being . . . and if God decreed that a person should be either righteous or wicked, or if there was some force inherent within his nature which irresistibly drew him to a certain course [or placed him under some form of duress] . . . by what right or justice could God punish the wicked or reward the righteous?"

8. In the *Hilchos Yesodei Hatorah* (Laws concerning the Basic Principles of the Torah 5:4), the Rambam writes that one who is threatened with death if he fails to commit a sin has "committed a transgression under duress" and

Therefore, if a person does not give to *tzedakah* because another person places him under duress (i.e., a threat to one's life if a donation is made), the individual is not punished for failing to give. However, incitement is not the same as the defense of duress, since everyone turns toward good or evil, and the legal or illegal in a spontaneous way, of his own volition. Since all have free will, nobody is under the duress of any inclination: rather, each is free to accept the advice, encouragement, and incitement of either his good or evil inclination.[9]

This distinction between incitement and duress is clearly recognized in Anglo-American criminal law. Duress is an established defense in law, and since the case is not one involving free will, the defendant is

---

continues that he will not be sentenced to death by the Court "even if, he committed murder ... then how much more so [is there a defence of duress in regard to other sins." Although one does something very negative when undertaking any sin, if this sin was performed under any form of duress, the "villain" is deemed a "victim," and suffers no punishment.

Thus, a clear paradox has arisen. The Rambam stated earlier that every Jew desires to do mitzvot, and only ever commits a sin when he is "incited by his evil inclination" and his true will is under its control. Therefore if the Rambam subsequently holds that "duress is a defence" to any sin, and that no Jew is punished when he commits a crime under duress, how can any Jew ever be liable for punishment? It appears that the Rambam is awarding any Jew the most perfect legal defence, since when he is faced by any criminal charge, a Jew can simply claim "my sin was done under the duress of my evil inclination; so I plead the defence of duress."

9. See *Sefer Hisvadiyus* 5746, vol. 3 (Kfar Chabad: Lahak Hanochos, 1987), pp. 321–322.

acquitted without punishment. However, if a defendant claims he has been incited by another, the court will not recognize this as any defense whatsoever.[10]

This answers the question as to why a "wicked" individual is included among a list of "givers to charity." It is clearly his inner will to give, but he has been temporarily incited to refrain from doing so. He may have no valid legal defense for his omission to give, but he should also have no fear that this "temporary" lapse of activity will separate him from his "giving" brothers.

A FLOATING EXCHANGE RATE

An atheist, a Catholic, and a Jew were discussing their various attitudes toward giving charity. "If money comes my way," explained the atheist, "I keep it. After all, no one is demanding it from me."

"I myself," said the Catholic, "believe that one has to be righteous with one's possessions; therefore, out of all the money which comes to me, I set aside half for myself, and give half to God."

"As for me," said the Jew, "I feel that I owe everything to God, so when I get any money, I immediately throw it all up to the heavens. Naturally, any money that God does not grab for Himself, I keep. . . ."

Although a minority of Jews may find ways in which to "escape" their *tzedakah* obligations, *Avos* lists

---

10. The court will simply ask the defendant "Who incited you to commit this crime?" and subsequently charge that named inciter with committing an inchoate (preliminary) offense, and this later case will have no effect upon the punishment of the original defendant.

the "four types of givers"[11] (even though the fourth
avoids giving), in order to include every individual.
Thus, even those who currently fail to donate sufficiently should be inspired by the fact that Jewish ethics
perceives their omission as based upon "temporary
incitement," and so does not omit them from its reg-
ister of "givers."

---

11. One possible explanation for the fact that the Mishnah states that "There are *four* types . . . ," when the reader
is clearly able to count the attitudes themselves, is in order
to equate the individuals, and indicate a common denominator: namely, the potential for improvement. One may
have thought that the highest level allows one to remain
contented with piety; yet the Mishnah is thus stating that
just as the lowest level requires development, so do all the
others.

This also explains why the entire discussion is included in *Ethics of the Fathers*, when *tzedakah* appears to
be more of an issue of law. By emphasizing the common
denominator of a need for improvement in the donations
to charity of all Jews, the Mishnah is making a statement
that is clearly ethical in character.

10

The Charitable Veil

The ambitions of Aron Salomon, a shoemaker in London's Jewish East End at the turn of the century, set legal history. As a result of incorporating his small business into a limited company, Aron Salomon was no longer liable for any of its debts, even though it was still in effect his business.[1] Consequently, the Salomon case brought down a "corporate veil" between Mr. Salomon and "his" company, so that when his company went bankrupt, he was not held financially responsible. The English court maintained that it was simply interested in the facts, in the activity which had been undertaken rather than in its motivation. The court wanted to know *what* had been done, rather than *why* it had been done.

Similarly, the Anglo-American laws of charity have no interest in "intention." The motives of the giver (whether for the purpose of tax-avoidance, social status, etc.) are wholly irrelevant to the legality of the donation, since the law only concerns itself with the

---

1. Salomon v Salomon (1895) H.L. Cases & C.A.

suitability of the beneficiary.[2] Thus, to be a "charity giver" in law, one need only do the *deed* of giving. A "veil" is then brought down over one's intentions and the law asks no further questions.

However, in Judaism, where so much emphasis is placed upon intention (*kavanah*), one would clearly expect that the thoughts of the donor when performing the mitzvah of *tzedakah* would be awarded an essential role. Although charity is a very "physical" deed, it would still be presumed that the mitzvah would succeed or fail on the quality of the motivations, aspirations, and intentions of the giver.

THE WILL TO DO

A Jewish law is an illustration of God's intention that a man perform a specific action.[3] However the question arises as to whether God's will is that a man perform the mitzvah combined with his human inten-

---

2. Pemsels Case (1891) A.C. 531. Lord McNaughten defined the "four headings" of worthy beneficiaries: those who (a) Relieve Poverty, (b) Advance Education, (c) Advance Religion, and (d) Fulfil other purposes that benefit the community.

3. Jewish law is Divinely commanded, and consequently displays the will of God. Therefore, when certain philosophies attempt to bring down a "veil" between Jewish law and the Will of God by rationalizing it and suggesting that certain deeds simply do not make intellectual sense, it should be recognized that such a division does not exist. Since intellect is subservient to will, one should not be disheartened if a specific law is difficult to intellectually justify; it is simply the desire of God Himself that the deed be done.

tions. Is it the thought that counts, or is the deed the most important thing? As regards the giving of *tzedakah*, the most extreme example of the "deed supercedes intention" philosophy would be the case where a person were to drop a coin from his pocket. If this coin was subsequently found by a poor man, would the dropped coin constitute a charitable donation in Jewish law? If this were so, it would mean that "deed" played such a vital role in Judaism, that one could perform a mitzvah without intending to, and without even knowing one had done so.

THE FIERCE OPPONENT

After the Giving of the Law at Mount Sinai, the Jewish People were led through the desert toward the Land of Canaan (Israel), and despite the fact that they were divided into twelve tribes, they were united under the leadership of Moses and his brother Aaron. Upon reaching the border of Canaan, Moses proposed that a leader of each tribe be sent as a spy into the Land in order to determine the most effective way to achieve its possession. The subsequent reports of the spies proved to be one of the most shocking episodes in Jewish history.

Ten of the twelve spies returned from Canaan with the news that "the land consumes its inhabitants . . . the people are fierce . . . and they are stronger than we are."[4] According to the Talmud,[5] the spies actually reported, "the people are fierce . . . and they are stronger than He [God] is"—an interpretation that ultimately transforms pessimism into blasphemy.

---

4. Num. 13:32.
5. *Sotah* 35a.

Although some Biblical commentators explain
that the Canaanites were Giants, and much stronger
than the previously-defeated Egyptians, how could the
ten spies presume them to be stronger than God Himself. The Jews had witnessed the ten plagues against
Pharaoh and Egypt, and they had seen the Red Sea split
for them and cover their pursuers. In fact, after they
witnessed the drowning of the Egyptian army, the Jews
sang a song of praise to God, which included the words,
"All the inhabitants of Canaan are melted away."[6] In
the desert, they had beaten all opposition, been fed by
the heavenly manna, and heard the voice of God at the
foot of Mount Sinai. How is it possible that the spies
could harbor any doubts as to the infinite power of
God? Irrespective of the military might of the armies
of Canaan, the reports of the ten spies do not seem to
make any sense.

The "sin" of the spies is often deemed as a lack of
appreciation for the miracles that had preceded, and
a clear ignorance of God's strength. However, any
simple denunciation of the spies must be condemned
as superficial and inaccurate, as they were all leaders
of their tribes, and consequently worthy of the appellation *Tzaddikim* (totally righteous).[7] There is clearly no
way that a *tzaddik* would, under any circumstances,
doubt the infinite power of God or fail to appreciate
his might.

In addition, the two spies who brought back favorable reports, Joshua and Caleb, did not refer to the
numerous miracles in Egypt or the Desert; and it is

---

6. Exod. 15:15.

7. See commentary of Rashi to Numbers 13:3, where
it is explained that the Torah refers to the spies as *Anashim*,
a term of great respect.

clear that the ten spies were not troubled by the extent of God's strength. So, if the spies were righteous and understood God's omnipotence, why did they sin by emphasizing the invincibility of their opposition?

A LAND THAT CONSUMES

The sin of the spies was less a fear of the giant Canaanites than a fear of the land itself.[8] While they remained in the desert, the Jewish people had all their physical needs taken care of: they had their food descending from Heaven in the form of the manna, they had continual water from the "Well of Miriam," and all their laundry was done by the "clouds of glory"[9]— the perfect "Welfare State." They were consequently able to devote all their time and energy to matters of spirituality, learning Torah, and relating to God. Entering the Land of Canaan would require physical labor of the land, and would drain the energy that was previously used for the spiritual. So the spies concluded that "the Land consumes its inhabitants." They clearly believed that living in a physical land would "consume" the spirituality of the inhabitant Jews and diminish their service to God.

GURU!

The elderly Jewish lady decided to start going to yoga classes. Week after week she would attend, but showed no real interest in the classes, and simply sat at the back of the room with her knitting.

---

8. *Likutei Sichos*, vol. 4, 6th ed. (KPS, 1992), p. 1041.
9. *Mechilta, Beshalach* 13:21: Midrash *Rabbah* 1:2.

Finally, after the course was completed, she amazed all present by signing up for the advanced course in Eastern meditation and faithfully attended every class, without showing the slightest interest. Having completed this course also, a trip to India to meet the Head Guru was offered and she immediately accepted.

When the elderly Jewish lady arrived at the foot of the mountain where the Guru lived, she was amazed to see thousands of people in line and horrified to hear that it was a three-week wait before she could see the Guru. "Unless you want to go in the Express line," she was told, "that will take just two hours, but you are only allowed to say three words to the Guru."

She immediately accepted, and after two hours of waiting, the Jewish lady was standing before the head Guru at the top of his mountain, and with her three word allowance, she simply pleaded, "Dovid, come home!"

Jews have always been a spiritual people, and the desert environment, full of miracles to provide all material necessities, was totally idyllic. The spies appreciated this opportunity to rise above the physical, and thus had great fears about entering a mundane environment. They believed that "the land" would consume much, if not all, of their vitality to serve God in a spiritual manner.

Yet, having discovered their true motives, it becomes unclear as to exactly what was their sin. The spies desired the best possible conditions to learn Torah and serve God. They were righteous and lofty individuals who genuinely cared for their people and sought only the religious and the spiritual: with such pure motives, and such sensible fears, what was their mistake, and why is the spirituality quest of the spies deemed "sinful"?

MORE MR. NICE GUY

The "emotionless miser" was famous for refusing to donate a single penny to charity, and for displaying no pity or compassion toward the poor. He was, however, troubled by his condition, and couldn't understand why he was so unable to feel any emotion for another human being.

However, during a particularly strong winter snowstorm, he was looking out of his window, and saw a poor old man lying in the snow, freezing to death. The emotionless miser felt pity. As he reached for some money and a warm coat, he suddenly realized that for the first time in his life, he was having an emotion for another individual. Consequently the miser became very excited. He had succeeded in changing his nature, and he could barely control his joy: so much so that he completely forgot about the old man outside, who subsequently froze to death.

It is clear that thinking "good" and feeling pity is not sufficient. To do good is what counts: the deed is the most important thing. This was the mistake of the spies, to totally misunderstand the purpose of life. Their perception of life's meaning was to elevate the soul of the individual by spirituality; they were wrong. The meaning of life is, rather, the sanctification of the physical world. This requires actual deeds, like feeding and clothing a poor, frozen man, not just feeling pity for him. One must be involved in the mundane and the physical, and through one's actions, make it holy. The mistake of the spies was to perceive a mitzvah as something spiritual and supernatural. In truth, a mitzvah is to take the natural and sanctify it.

The spies pulled down a "veil" between the physical and the spiritual, without understanding that each only has purpose when combined with the other. They did not comprehend that their task was to enter Canaan, to use the tools that they had acquired during their life of holiness in the desert, and to inject that inspiration into everyday life. The mistake of the spies is fundamental, because it contradicts the very reason why God created the world.

THE DESIRE TO DWELL

Much philosophizing and speculation surrounds the purpose of the creation of the world. Yet for a Jew, a clear answer is to be found in the Torah. The world was created because God "desired a dwelling place down below."[10] In his *Textbook of Chassidic Philosophy*, the Alter Rebbe explains that this "dwelling place" is prepared through physical mitzvahs, through actual deeds."[11] It is specifically in this world, where He is so concealed, that God's desire to reside finds expression, and it is clear that He will only reside where He feels comfortable and welcome. Thus it is explained that Divine comfort is ensured by fulfilling mitzvahs, the Divine Will. As to why this is God's desire, the Alter Rebbe simply answers that "on a desire, you cannot ask any questions!" Thus, it is clear that by the simple fulfilment of tangible, physical mitzvahs, one fulfils the very purpose of creation.[12]

---

10. Midrash *Tanchuma, Nasso* 7:1.

11. *Tanya* (*Likutei Amarim*), Ch. 36-7.

12. Even though there are other reasons stated in the Torah for the purpose of creation, Chassidic thought demonstrates that the physical activity of mitzvahs is the most central purpose. See *Likutei Sichos*, vol. 20, 2nd ed. (KPS, 1989), pp. 283-285.

Therefore, the means by which this world becomes a place in which God wants to reside is through physical mitzvahs. Good deeds are the ultimate purpose of creation, whereas spirituality, meditating in a desert, and denigrating the mundane are the antithesis of a purposeful existence. The ten spies did not appreciate that the miracles and spiritualism of their desert experience were merely a preparation for their entry into Canaan.

The spies argued that "the Land consumes its inhabitants," and this was not despite the previous miracles, but because of them. The spies feared that without these desert miracles, which awarded them the opportunity to concentrate solely on what they perceived to be the service of God, they would be forced to leave the ethereal realms, and have to descend to the natural world. To cross the River Jordan was to enter a world without miracles, to become part of the natural, physical world; their purpose was not to be consumed by the physical, but rather to sanctify it, to refine it and make it holy. In emphasizing the primacy of the lofty, the thoughtful, and the religious, the spies erred badly, and failed in both their mission as spies and as Jews.

ACTIONS COUNT

When discussing God's "dwelling place," the Alter Rebbe distinguishes between the mitzvahs of thought, with those of action.[13] He recommends mitzvahs of action, as the principal means by which the world is sanctified, and advocates the deed as the tool for infusing the material with holiness.

---

13. [and speech]—*Tanya* (*Likutei Amarim*), Ch. 4.

Consequently, a "veil" is brought down and a distinction made between *tzedakah* and all other mitzvahs, as *tzedakah* is deemed the best tool for fulfilling
one's purpose in life, since it is the ultimate mitzvah
of action. No other mitzvah succeeds in introducing
so much holiness into so much of the mundane. When
one gives *tzedakah*, he does not only make physical
money holy, but he also makes holy every physical
object and every moment of time and ounce of energy
which was used for the acquisition of the donated sum.
The donor does a deed that elevates himself, his business, his employer or employees, his suppliers and his
customers. The deed is the most important thing, and
the deed of *tzedakah* elevates more of the corporeal
world, than any other mitzvah.

Having understood the primacy of action within
Jewish law, one would be less startled by the revelation that an individual who drops a coin, which is later
found by a poor man *does* successfully perform a
mitzvah.[14] The commandment of *tzedakah* is "to give
to the poor and to enliven them," and if the action of
dropping a coin succeeds in achieving this result, then
the loser of the coin becomes the gainer of a mitzvah.
To conclude that one can actually perform the mitzvah
of giving to charity without ever realizing it, is clearly
the perfect illustration of the prominence of the deed.

CONTRIBUTORS ANONYMOUS

The millionaire made a specific request that his donation be anonymous, and was greeted with nothing but
commendation. However a problem arose when the

------

14. Lev. 5:17—Rashi quoting Sifri.

beneficiary examined the check, and discovered that it had not been signed. The subsequent complaint was met with the words, "How else can I make sure it is anonymous?"

Although the check was for a very large sum, to a very worthy cause and given in a very noble manner; it was no donation at all. The deed of giving *tzedakah* had not been performed.

Other problems may arise with anonymous giving, as many people may conclude, that if a certain individual does not appear to give *tzedakah*, "and he is very rich," they may well be inspired to refrain from giving themselves. Therefore, even though it is necessary to "walk modestly with God," and giving large sums publicly, may well cause arrogance, R. Moshe Isserles (Rema, 1520–1572) rules that it is "fitting to publicize a mitzvah."[15] Thus, if one wants to give anonymously, it is advisable that he still give some money publicly. This is because others may be discouraged from giving, when they mistakenly presume that the anonymous giver does not give, and the giver himself, may also lose the advantage of the "social pressure" to maintain and increase his charitable donations.

For those who may be worried that public donations may lead to an increase in their level of arrogance, they should remember the story of R. Sholom Dov Ber (the Mittler Rebbe, 1773–1827), whose Chassidim would remit his teachings on their way back from the village of Lubavitch. One particular Chassid complained to the Mittler Rebbe that since he was a particularly good teacher, he felt much pride when he taught, and was worried that he might be becoming arrogant. He therefore enquired as to whether he should

---

15. *Shulchan Aruch, Yoreh Deah* 249-13.

refrain from teaching. The Mittler Rebbe's answer was, "Even if you become an *Onion,* you should continue to teach."

This means that "you" are not the most important thing, when you are doing a mitzvah. What is important, is that the mitzvah gets done. Similarly with *tzedakah*: whether one becomes arrogant by the publicizing of his name, if it will benefit the poor, it should be done. Appropriate advice for those who seek humility is not to connect their giving of *tzedakah* and its publicization with this noble aspiration: they should continue to give, in large amounts and publicly, and simultaneously refine themselves and their character traits to limit arrogance. Ultimately, the poor are really interested in the quality of the gift rather than the qualities of the giver.

The donor is judged on his actions, not his thoughts. It is his actions which fulfil his purpose in creation, and so Judaism brings down a "veil" between his thought and his deed, concentrating clearly on the latter. Since the deed is the most important thing, and *tzedakah* is the mitzvah which is more based upon action than any other, the Jerusalem Talmud justifiably awards it the epithet of "The Mitzvah."

11
Lifting the Veil to Reveal a Smiling Face

The unprecedented *chutzpah* of Aron Salomon, to bring down a "veil" between himself and his company, and consequently to avoid financial liability, led to countless other schemes of veiling managerial intention. Since the courts had announced that they were interested in deed rather than intention, directors of companies undertook numerous acceptable activities for a variety of dubious intentions. However, to every precedent exceptions appear, and it was only a matter of time before the courts were forced to examine motivations and intentions. Ultimately, the courts were compelled to create the laws of "lifting the veil."[1]

---

1. Other names for this procedure include "piercing" or "penetrating" the corporate veil, etc. For a detailed analysis of the variety of methods for "lifting," see the classic article of Professor Ottolenghi of the Hebrew University, "From Peeping behind the Corporate Veil, to Ignoring It Completely" (M.L.R.1990. 53:338).

While recognizing the primacy of deeds over intentions, the courts deemed a number of companies to be "fraudulent," "facades," or "mere puppets of their creators": the veil between company and manager had to be lifted, and the motives of the architects of a facade company were deemed highly relevant. The company and its "deeds" were still the primary thing, but the management and their "motives" could no longer be veiled and ignored.

This state of affairs seems to parallel Jewish law, since the quality of one's donation is clearly improved by the manner in which the money is given: but a body of laws that are fundamentally based upon actions would not at first glance place much emphasis upon intentions, manners, and motivations. Judaism, in its orientation toward action, draws down a veil between deed and intention; however, are there any circumstances where that veil must be lifted? Having established that mitzvahs are predicated on activity, to what extent (if any) does intention play a role?

The Rambam writes in the *Laws of the Poor* that, "All who give to *tzedakah* with a miserable face, which looks to the ground; even if he gives one hundred gold coins, he has lost his merit for the mitzvah."[2] The whole realm of motivations for mitzvahs thus appears of paramount importance. The incident with the twelve spies illustrated that God is interested in tangible, physical actions rather than spiritual and noble motivations; but the whole area of intention *(kavanah)* in mitzvahs has been dramatically re-emphasized by this simple law in the Rambam. Having concluded the previous chapter by advocating the primacy of deed in Jewish law, based principally upon the historical incident with the twelve spies, it appears that the

---

2. Rambam, *Hilchos Matanos L'aniyim* 10:4.

Rambam's promotion of intention acts as a powerful counterbalance to that conclusion.

EQUALITY IN ACTION

One week after the Torah reading describing the "sin" of the spies (*Shlach*), the portion (*Korach*) which follows details a fierce revolution against Moses.[3] The principal complaint which Korach had was against the leadership of Moses and his brother, Aaron, and particularly the authority for Aaron to be the *Kohen Gadol* (spiritual leader) of the Jewish people. However, Aaron had assumed that position over one year before, and so the timing of Korach's complaint is suspicious.

The reason for this strange delay is provided by the incident with the twelve spies. Korach waited until the "sin" of the spies, because it was Moses's response to the spies that inspired Korach's grievance. The mistake of the spies was in their desire to be elevated from the physical world, so that the mundanity of the "land" of Israel would not inhibit or consume their "desert" spirituality.[4] Consequently, Moses's reply to the spies was that the deed is the most important thing, and that a real connection with God can only come about by the active performance of mitzvahs. It was, ironically, with this very answer that Korach built up the case for his "prosecution" against Moses and Aaron.

Although, from the perspective of Torah learning and spirituality, there was a profound difference in the relative merits of Moses and Korach,[5] nevertheless

---

3. *Seder Olam, Rabbah* 8; Rashbam and Tosafos on *Bava Basra* 119a.

4. See chapter 10, above.

5. *Eruvin* 54b.

from the view of "the priority of the deed," it would appear that both of them were equal. The donation of a single coin by Moses is not, at first glance, any different to a donation by Korach, and since the "priority of the deed" was only appreciated after the incident with the spies, Korach had no grounds for complaint until after that time. Korach accepted that Moses and Aaron were on a much higher level in Torah learning and in the intention (*kavanah*) with which they performed their mitzvahs. Yet his complaint of "Why have you elevated yourselves?"[6] refers to the physicality of mitzvahs, which supposedly renders all Jews equal. The complaint consequently came one year after the elevation of Aaron, since it was not until then that the Jews became fully aware of the fact that the deed is the most important thing: it was in this respect that Moses and Aaron appeared equal to all other Jews, ultimately giving Korach cause for dissent.

Korach argued "All Jews are equally holy," and protested the ultimate authority of those who sought to rule. If the criteria for the differentiation of individuals is at the level of the physical, active part of the mitzvah, then all Jews appear genuinely equal: Korach's case thus appears proven.

However, Korach was one of the 150 leaders of the Jewish nation at that time, and was also from the tribe of Levi, which was considered the most eminent of the twelve tribes. Korach therefore appears to advocate the Orwellian view that "All [Jews] are equal, but some are more equal than others."

It is even clear from much of Korach's conduct, that it is not the position of Priest which he objected to, but rather the fact that it was granted to Aaron rather than himself. A certain degree of hypocrisy thus

---

6. Num. 16:3.

becomes apparent, as Korach only argues "all Jews are equally holy" (based upon the philosophy that "the deed is the most important thing"), in order to usurp the power of those above him.

A MINOR CASE OF TREASON

To condemn Korach as merely a hypocrite who adopts arguments, only to further his own power is somewhat simplistic. His basic philosophy is best understood, when it is appreciated that Korach's most intense and deep-rooted abhorrence was for the "political position" of Moses. The Talmud describes Moses' authority as "like that of a King"[7] and thus elevates his position to that of supreme leader, rather than a mere representative or delegate of the people. Korach is more accurately described as an "Anti-Monarchist" in the sense that he accepts the need for some type of "democratic" leadership, however his contention that the whole community is holy precludes the role of a supreme leader like Moses. All are comparable in the Jewish community, according to Korach's understanding, and so the position of Absolute Monarch is untenable, since it places one individual upon an incomparably high pedestal, above the entire people.[8]

---

7. *Zevachim* 102a.

8. If Moses's position would have been more of a delegate/representative for the Jews, Korach would not have had any valid complaint. Also, before the incident with the spies, the position of a monarch, based on the Greek notion of a "Philosopher-King" may have been defensible: "whoever understands the most [Jewish and Torah] philosophy, merits the position of King." However, according to the "primacy of deeds" approach, which was introduced

The relationship of an Absolute Monarch to his subjects is unique, in that there is a quantum leap in status for one who becomes king. The Talmud[9] describes the total subservience that is necessary toward a monarch, when it relates the narrative of the King's subject who simply made a minor motioning action in the presence of his King, and was consequently deprived of his life. The simple motioning was deemed to be "High Treason," illustrating that one's very existence can be connected to that of one's ruler.

In a modern and "enlightened" society, we appear contented with republicanism and figurehead Monarchies, and the very notion of the "off-with-his-head" type ruler is seen as a historical anachronism, which "progress" has left far behind. Yet, this clarion cry of "Liberty, Equality, Fraternity" appears entirely consistent with the view of Korach: if "all are equally holy," there is no place in society for an effective monarchy. How could Moses possibly defend himself against this seemingly genuine search for equality? If Moses could tell the spies that a world of action is what God desires, how could he respond to accusations that in such a world, all are equal, and his position is unacceptable?

A VERY SHINY DWELLING PLACE

Moses's response was characteristically profound. He simply answered Korach's accusations with the words

---

at the time of the spies, even "Torah Philosophy" is secondary to physical mitzvahs, and an absolutist Monarch could not be chosen for his deeds, since at this level "all Jews are equally holy."

9. *Hagigah* 5b.

"Wait until morning, and God will make it known that which is His and who is holy."[10] Although it appears a somewhat weak response, Moses achieved the complete refutation of Korach's entire argument. Moses was not procrastinating or merely "buying time" when he recommended waiting "until morning": he was qualifying and illuminating the original philosophy that "the deed is the most important thing," a view which Korach's attack was wholly relying upon.[11]

GOOD DEEDS IN THE MUD

Korach's ideology was, to a certain degree, the precursor to Sartre's philosophy of Existentialism, that "man is defined solely by his actions . . . Existentialism tells him that hope lies only in action, and that the only thing that allows man to live is action."[12] Although this view of the primacy of deed was advocated by Moses to the spies, Korach took it to an illogical extreme and

---

10. Num. 16:5.

11. The classic Biblical commentator Rashi attempts to explain Moses's answer by suggesting: (a) Moses wanted to wait, so that Korach could do *teshuvah*, and (b) He wanted to display that just as God made distinctions between night and day, so too would He distinguish between Korach and Aaron. However, the difficulties with these two explanations are that (a) Korach could do *teshuvah* at any time, including that evening, and (b) Moses could also show the Divine distinction between day and night by scheduling his "showdown" at night. It is thus not entirely clear as to how "wait until morning" succeeds in refuting Korach's denunciation.

12. Sartre, *L'existentialisme est un Humanisme* (Paris 1946).

failed to appreciate that a physical mitzvah could be done in a manner that was "not good."

Although a mitzvah is a Divine command, and thus has the virtue of connecting its doer with the infinite Creator, it consequently possesses the flaw of being dependent upon its human doer. It is thus possible to do a mitzvah for a multitude of motivations that are "not kosher." This is analogous to a diamond which is covered in mud, so that it fails to achieve its purpose—to shine and illuminate a room. Such a diamond even achieves the very opposite of its purpose, it actually absorbs light. Similarly, a mitzvah which is performed for a dubious motive may not only fail to produce a Godly light, but may result in the absorbing of the Divine light within the world, and thus add strength to the world's negativity.[13]

The fact that even within the active mitzvahs there can be "mitzvahs as positive deeds" and "mitzvahs as negative deeds" appears to nullify Korach's call of "equality in activity." Although the mitzvahs of Jews are equal, in the sense that they are all the will of God, and are thus "like diamonds," Korach's argument is refuted as "some of these mitzvahs are diamonds covered with mud."[14]

If one were to follow the "existentialism" of the post-spies era, and suggest that all that really counts is one's deeds, then whether or not a mitzvah is "like a shining diamond" is not so important; however, the fact that non-shining mitzvahs actually add strength to the forces of negativity within the world, is evidence

---

13. *Likutei Sichos*, vol. 4, 6th ed. (KPS, 1992), p. 1053.

14. The reason Jewish Law recommends that even those with dubious motives should learn and do mitzvahs is that through *teshuvah*, the mud will disappear and the inner diamond will be revealed.

that one must worry about intentions *(kavanah)* when performing a mitzvah. It also illustrates that even in the world of action, some are more equal than others.

Through physical mitzvahs, one is able to accommodate God in this lowly world. However God "desires" a place in which to dwell, a place which is revealed, comfortable, and shining: thus, the need for mitzvahs to be "shiny" is a prerequisite.

Moses's answer to Korach was that although you are correct when you proclaim that the deed is the most important thing, you are forgetting about the importance of the quality of that deed. The mitzvah should be done, according to Moses, "until morning"—until it is bright, until it shines and illuminates the world. Mitzvahs should be done with good intentions: they should be diamonds without mud.[15]

In fact, Moses's greatest quality was actually in the world of action, rather than in that of intellect, intentions, and Torah learning. Since his mitzvahs were of such a shining nature, Moses was able to teach the Jews who were already doing mitzvahs how they could achieve qualitatively. He was able to illustrate how

------

15. Rashi is also more readily understood since: (a) Although *teshuvah* is possible at night (this is the lower level of returning to God which is based upon fear), Moses recommends *teshuvah* in the manner of "morning," a light, revealed *teshuvah* which is based upon love of God, and which will wash away the "mud" that rests upon any existing diamonds; and (b) The fact that God distinguishes between day and night, and consequently between Korach and Moses, is best illustrated by the choice of morning. Moses illustrated that God distinguishes between "Shiny" and "tarnished" mitzvahs, and although it is true that "all Jews are holy," as each Jew is filled with mitzvahs, Moses was worthy of his monarchical position since his mitzvahs were "like morning," they were incomparably shinier.

they could "wash away" the mud from their existing diamonds, and also guarantee a "bright" future.

A SHINING EXAMPLE

It is clear that any argument that "it's the thought that counts" and that "it's possible to be a good Jew at heart" is fallacious after the episode of the spies. Pitying the poor is not *tzedakah*: feeding them is. However, the incident with Korach illustrates that it is a comparable fallacy to advocate that "all that counts is the deed": Moses's answer of "wait until morning" proved that mitzvahs must be shiny, they must be refined. Therefore, as the Rambam holds "all who give *tzedakah* with a miserable face . . . lose their merit for the mitzvah." While the deed of charity must be done in a tangible manner, the poor will be affected in many cases by the quality of the gift, by the way it is given, as well as the amount. Accordingly, a smiling face has the power to totally transform the mitzvah of *tzedakah*.[16]

---

16. This was clear even before the incidents with the spies and Korach. When the Jews left Egypt, they took with them "all the spoils of Egypt," and at the parting of the Red Sea, they acquired even more riches from their drowned pursuers. It is thus necessary to inquire as to how such a wealthy people could perform the mitzvah of *tzedakah*, when each of them was rich? The wealthy actually need the poor, in order to perform the mitzvah of *tzedakah*, so how can it be performed when there are none who have financial needs to be filled?

The simple answer is that the Jews continued to perform acts of *tzedakah*, without money. A smiling face alone was sufficient *tzedakah*, and thus general acts of kindness were able to make the desert shine.

The veil between the actual deed of *tzedakah* and the intentions, motivations, and manner in which it is given has reached the stage where it must be lifted: underneath, the mitzvah demands an open hand, a shiny coin, and a smiling face.

12

The Sun Shines
on the Poor

The basic definition of economics in the definitive textbook by Samuelson and Nordhaus is wrong. "Economics—the study of how people choose to employ
scarce resources,"[1] is a definition which accepts the
basic "theory of scarcity," that the world contains a
limited number of resources.

Yet in his innovative publication, *Unlimited Wealth:
The Theory and Practice of Economic Alchemy*,[2] the Jewish economist Paul Zane Pilzer argues that the world
is a virtual cornucopia of resources. He asserts that a
society's wealth is determined by its unlimited human
ingenuity, which constantly redefines that which constitutes a resource. In the nineteenth century, as the
supply of whale blubber shrank, humankind discovered oil and natural gas. Today, the most important

---

1. Paul Samuelson and William D. Nordhaus, *Economics*, 12th ed. (New York: McGraw Hill, 1985), p. 4.
2. New York: Crown Publishers, 1991.

141

technology is made out of the world's most common material, silicon, which is basically sand.

So wealth is not limited, suggests Pilzer, "it is as unlimited as the power of our minds." This reinforces the view that a world in which each individual is wealthy appears the most appropriate creation of an all powerful and benevolent God. Yet, throughout the world poverty remains widespread.

THE GREATER NEED OF A GREATER NUMBER

The tragedy of world poverty appears to powerfully contradict Albert Einstein's philosophy that "God does not play dice." A "Divine plan" which allows for such hardship and poverty[3] is actually the work of God, so his appellation the "All-Merciful" appears somewhat difficult to appreciate. Since everything is by Divine providence, a Jew is obligated to attempt an understanding as to why the Divine awards so many millions of His creations, such a miserable providence.

Even if, for some reason, there have to be poor people within society, it would have been preferable for the poor to receive their sustenance directly from

---

3. "Poverty is more difficult than fifty plagues" (*Bava Basra* 116a). This is not mere hyperbole, but based upon the lament of the prophet Job: "Pity me, you who are my friends, for the hand of God has touched me [with poverty]." Therefore, the Talmud asserts, "If the finger of God administered upon the Egyptians their ten plagues (Exodus 8:15), the hand of God which touched Job with poverty, administered upon him fifty plagues." However, while the extent of Job's suffering may have been somewhat unique, his miserable financial position was not.

God, rather than from other human beings.[4] Instead, the way in which the world is set up today ensures that, not only do the poor have to beseech their Creator and pray from the depths of their heart that He help them, but having done that, they then have to beg from their fellowman. Why did God burden them with this extra effort and responsibility which seems so unfair and unnecessary?

One of the answers to this question is given in the Midrash[5] which states that when a person makes a charitable donation, the favor which the poor man does for him by accepting is "greater than the favor which he does for the poor man by giving." God created *tzedakah* in order to provide the world's "givers" with the opportunity to be benevolent. If everyone was equal, and one human being was not dependent upon another, then there would be little need for acts of kindness. So *tzedakah* was created *for the sake of the giver*, that he may have the opportunity to perform an act of beneficence, and make the world a more beautiful place.

DO IT YOURSELF

Yet, it is clear that God did not need to create poverty, and He could easily have sustained the destitute Him-

---

4. Since God has decided that there have to be poor people, why could His plan not have been that the poor should have to pray? So that if they fail to pray and beseech convincingly to Him, they do not get a sufficient livelihood. However, if their prayers are deemed heartfelt and sincere, then God will grant them all the money that they require.

5. *Vayikra Rabbah*, ch. 34, v. 8.

self. The Midrash may state that if there were no poor
people, there would be no opportunity to give, but since
God is infinitely wise, surely He could have found a way
to give all the benefits and all the beauty which benevolence and giving adds to the world, without resorting
to the need for poverty? Logic may well dictate that
tzedakah requires there to be a needy beneficiary, but
God Himself is not limited by the rules of logic.

An alternative explanation is proposed in another
Midrash.[6] To King David's supplication as to why a
benevolent God chose not to create a world where
everybody was rich, God replied, "If I had made a
world of equality, how could there be kindness, how
could truth exist?" The commentators explain that God
is asking, "How could I create a world in which the
concept of *tzedakah* does not exist?"

This Midrash is proclaiming that the creation of
the world in the manner of rich and poor, is not merely
so that the rich have the opportunity to give; but is due
to an *intrinsic greatness* in the mitzvah of *tzedakah*
itself. The act of sustenance itself must be so great, in
its own right, that God deems it worthy to create an
inequitable world. Poverty is neither for the sake of the
rich/giver or the poor/receiver, but for the sake of the
power of the mitzvah of *tzedakah* itself.[7]

With all its hardship and humiliation, poverty is
a creation which God would gladly have done without,
and it is a "very big price to pay" for an environment
in which charity can take place. From the perspective
of some form of "Divine cost-benefit analysis," is the
benefit of the mitzvah of *tzedakah* truly capable of
outweighing the tremendous cost of filling the world
with famine and indigence?

---

6. *Rabbah Mishpatim* 31
7. *Sefer HaMaamorim* 5688, "Ze Hayom," ch. 78.

MOONLIGHTING

The *Tikunei Zohar*[8] makes a comparison between the rich man and the sun, and between the poor man and the moon. Since the moon is not a source of light itself—it merely reflects the light of the sun—the light which it receives from the sun is considered to be the moon receiving *tzedakah.*

Yet, a problem arises when one examines the Jewish approach to the moon. While the calendar which most of the world uses is solar, and is based on the sun, the Jewish calendar bases itself on the lunar cycle, a cycle based on the growth of the moon. The fact that we increase the counting day by day should represent an increase in strength in the subject of the count. So, one would expect, that as we count upwards in the days of the month, the moon would be getting bigger all the time. However, from the fifteenth day of the month onwards, the moon gets smaller. Why is it that the Torah requires us to continue to count bigger while the moon is simultaneously diminishing into oblivion?

ELEMENTARY ASTRONOMY

The reason that the moon is not seen at the very beginning of the month is because it is so close to the sun that in the very presence of the sun's power the moon becomes insignificant, like a student who is humbled in the presence of a great teacher. There is simply nothing that the student could do in front of his teacher that would seem appropriate. Similarly, when the moon is very close to the sun, there is little or nothing the moon can offer which the sun could not. Therefore we do not

---

8. Ch. 44.

see the moon because it becomes humbled; totally nullified in comparison to the great source and luminary, the sun.[9]

However, as the days pass by the moon begins to move away from the sun. The more it moves away, the greater its presence can be noticed, because as it moves further away, it is less in the presence of its giver, of its superior and the source of its light, so it appears more of an independent entity. One observes the moon reflecting the light of the sun as a separate luminary in the sky, because it is no longer in such close proximity to the sun that it becomes insignificant.

This reaches a peak on the fifteenth day of the month, when there is a full moon—illustrating that the moon has reached such a state of independence that it is reflecting light perfectly, like a student who has learned everything that the teacher has to offer. The student has absorbed every piece of information which has been taught. He has understood and remembered, and is now able to answer any questions one might have on the teachings of his master—this is a full moon.

MORE THAN MEETS THE EYE

However, the sun has more to offer than its light. A full moon (on the fifteenth) displays that the moon is quite contented to receive all the light it can get. It enjoys its job of accepting, and this can be seen from the amount of light it reflects throughout the globe. However, the most desirable state of affairs would be if, ultimately, the moon/the recipient was able to become a giver. A true student, who has achieved his full potential, is not merely a student who has taken all that

9. Siddur Im D'Ach of the Alter Rebbe - 4.

his teacher has to offer, but the student who *becomes* a teacher.

In the scenario of the sun and the moon, a full moon may appear to be "full potential," yet it only means that the moon is now a perfect reflector. Even though it looks like the sun (it is large and round, and displays a large amount of light), nevertheless, it is still only a student, reflecting its Master, and has not yet learned how to give of its own.

However, in the second half of the month the moon learns how to be a giver, and having appreciated that "it is better to give than receive," it begins to act like its teacher, the sun. Consequently, we can continue to count upwards, because there is dramatic progress in the activity of the moon.

AN ESSENTIAL DATE

Many people are surprised when they read the statistics of divorce rates—particularly when comparing religious Jewish families with the rest of the world. One may think that the modern, secular way of meeting a partner would be the best approach. A "trial marriage," a boy lives with a girl for as long as possible, until they really get to know each other. Convinced that they have seen each other in every possible situation imaginable, and then certain that this is the person "who I love," they are assured that this marriage is going to last.

However, the Torah method is that after a relatively short meeting of the other person, namely five times, maybe ten or fifteen, the couple will have reached a decision upon marriage. This process appears somewhat strange, and yet what is even more outlandish is that these marriages are so much stronger and last so much longer. One only has to meet a few such families to see that the vast majority are flourishing, lively, and vibrant, and any question of stigma or "peer pressure" as the reason for the marriages' longevity is immediately discarded.

This "marital bliss" is explained by Chassidic philosophy, which refers to two parts of an individual. These two facets—"essence," who a person really is, deep down in his inner personality, and "appearance," how a person acts, how he looks, and behaves. While behavior and "appearance" are subject to change, "essence"—who a person really is—never changes.

So when one says to another under the wedding canopy, "I am going to stay with you for the next forty years," it means that whoever you are and whatever your "essence" is, I accept it. I may not know how you are going to behave for the next forty years, but I accept you for your "essence," from which all your "appearance" will subsequently emanate.

Therefore, when a person wants to date in order to get married, what has to be appreciated is that one is accepting the "essence," which one cannot see. Consequently, five or ten meetings should prove sufficient to determine that the other person's appearance and behavior are not displeasing. Since it is known that one is accepting the "essence" of the other person, there is no sense in spending five years dating, because you will still not appreciate or see the "essence" of the other person.

EVERYBODY WANTS TO GIVE THE WORLD

With the moon and the sun, it is clear that there is a very big difference between "essence" and "appearance." When there is a full moon, in the middle of the month, it means that the moon is like the sun, but only in "appearance." The "behavior" of the moon is big, round, and extremely shiny—exactly as the sun appears—but there is one thing the moon has not yet learned: it has failed to comprehend the sun's "essence." The moon must appreciate that the "essence" of the sun is the ability to give.

"Essence" is comparable to "darkness," since it can never be truly known, or realistically observed. So, when the moon gets smaller and "darker" in the second half of the month, it is getting closer and closer to the "essence" of the sun. This means that the moon is actually becoming a giver. The reason that we count upwards in the second half of the month is because the moon is now understanding and becoming that which the very essence of the sun represents.

REACHING THE ESSENCE

If God had created the world without *Tzedakah*, with no poor people with a need to receive, then everyone in the world would be a recipient from God. We would all experience the limitations of being a mere receiver (similar to the moon in the first half of the month). We could not reach "essence," meaning not only the essence of each other, but even the essence of God, since "essence" can only be appreciated when one is a giver.[10]

God created poverty for the sake of *tzedakah*, and he "required" *tzedakah* so that the concept of *essence* could enter the world. God "desires a dwelling place

---

10. *Sefer Hasichos* 5752/1992, vol. 1 (KPS, 1993), p. 158.

for his essence," which means he wants to exist "down here," not just in a manner of behavior or appearance, but he wants His *essence* to be revealed down in this world. God facilitates the mitzvah of *tzedakah*, in order that everyone can be a giver, relating to the very essence of God, which from the very beginning was the purpose of creation.

13

Taking an Interest
in the Poor

The seemingly impossible task of compiling a definitive list where different levels of gifts to *tzedakah* are ranked in a qualitative order was undertaken by the Rambam in his *Hilchos Matanos Aniyim* (*Laws of Gifts to the Poor*).[1] The Rambam quantifies eight distinct levels, which are (in descending order):

8. To give *tzedakah* with a miserable face.
7. To give a poor man less than a "proper" sum, but to do so with a cheerful demeanor.
6. To give *tzedakah* after the poor man has made a direct and specific request.
5. To give *tzedakah* before the poor man makes any request.
4. To give in such a manner that the poor man knows from whom his is receiving, but the giver is unaware of the identity of his beneficiary. (The Rambam compares this level to the "great amongst the Sages" who would place their *tzedakah* in a sheet

---

1. The list is set out in chap. 10, law 7.

"and throw it over their shoulders," so that the poor
could take anonymously.)

3. To give in a manner that prevents the poor man
   from becoming aware of the giver's identity. (The
   Rambam compares this level to the "great amongst
   the sages" who would leave the money secretly at
   the doors of the poor.)

2. To give *tzedakah* so that the giver does not know to
   whom he gives and the poor man does not know
   from whom he receives.

However, it is in level number 1., in the best quality gift to *tzedakah*, that all preconceived notions of
what constitutes a good gift to charity immediately
disappear. The highest rank, the best possible gift to
tzedakah, need not be a gift at all; it is "a donation, an
interest-free loan, or to go into a partnership with the
poor man . . . in order to strengthen his hand, so that
he will not need to beg from others."

GIVING MORE THAN MERE MONEY

Jewish law demands that every loan between two Jews
be "interest-free,"[2] so it is ironic that simply giving such
a "loan" could be deemed the highest form of "gift" to
charity. There is surely a greater degree of self-sacrifice
in giving over money for which one will never receive
a tangible return. When performing the mitzvah of
tzedakah, it may have been originally thought that a
gift would far supersede a loan in any ranking, and it
may even have been presumed that this "number
one," would not even have made it on to a list of "gifts
to *tzedakah*" at all.

---

2. See *Shulchan Aruch HaRav, Hilchos Ribbis*, vol. 4 (KPS,
1987), pp. 1548–1569; based upon Deut. 23:20.

The definition of "a gift" in law is where there is a transfer of property from the *promisor* to the *promisee*, and yet no benefit passes to the *promisor* and no detriment is felt by the *promisee*. In the scenario of an interest-free loan there is clearly a detriment to the *promisee* (the poor man), to the extent that the money passed over has to be returned at a later date. So, what is the aspect of an "interest-free loan" that makes it qualitatively superior to the giving of an unconditional free gift?

TOP OF THE LEAGUE

One approach would be to suggest that the feelings and the pride of the receiver have to be taken into consideration in any gift to *tzedakah*. Consequently, a loan is preferable, to the extent that the beneficiary walks away with his pride intact, and has the opportunity at a later date to repay the loan in full.

However the feelings of the beneficiary are merely one factor to be taken into consideration when ranking gifts to *tzedakah*, and so a "donation" (particularly if it is exactly the sum which the poor man requires, and if it is given before he has to even approach the giver) would appear a more generous and good deed than simply handing over money and simultaneously requesting its return at a later date. There must be something innately special about an interest-free loan which results in its "top ranking" in the "charitable donations league."

THE ADVICE OF POLONIUS

Tremendous praise for the interest-free loan would come as somewhat of a surprise to a Gentile, unfamiliar with Jewish law. This is due to the fact that the Oxford English Dictionary for centuries (and until relatively recently) defined a "Jew" as a "usurer—a miserly money lender for interest." From Shylock to the Rothschilds, Jews have always been famous for being outside the boundaries of the Christian laws of usury. In fact, prior to the Second World War the only non-Biblical Jews familiar to the Japanese were Shylock from Shakespeare's *The Merchant of Venice* and Jacob Schiff, an American moneylender. Schiff, frustrated by the Russian pogroms against the Jews, loaned the Japanese most of their money in their successful war against the Russians at the beginning of this century.

An interest-free loan is seen as the height of generosity in the Western world. Modern productions of *The Merchant of Venice*, in their determination to reverse centuries of anti-Semitism (which the play has depicted and provoked),[3] display Shylock's demand for "a pound of flesh" (the interest on his loan) to be nothing more than a mere joke. Consequently, the "three thousand ducat" loan becomes "interest free," and therefore the Jew Shylock is elevated from bloodthirsty usurer to highly generous benefactor.[4] Centuries of Jewish success as financiers clearly evidences that Jewish law does not prohibit a loan to a Gentile for interest. However such a transaction between two Jews is highly illegal in Jewish law, and is an offense by both

---

3. John Gross, *Shylock: A Legend and Its Legacy* (New York: Touchsone/Simon and Schuster, 1992). For analysis of anti-Semitism within the play, and historical ramifications.

4. See R. Shlomo Yosef Zevin z"l on the Jewish laws of interest relating to the loan of Shylock, *L'or Hahalachah* (*Mishpat Shylock*), *The Light of Jewish Law* (Jerusalem: Mosad Harav Kook, 1946).

the borrower and the lender.[5] So, it is evident that Judaism advocates the Polonius philosophy on interest, that "Neither a borrower, nor a lender, be" (*Hamlet*, Act I, Scene iii).

PLAGUED WITH DEBTS

The laws concerning interest are preceded by the words, "If your brother becomes impoverished . . . you shall strengthen him"[6] which is the legal source for the Rambam's highest level of *tzedakah*. The "charity" of an interest-free loan, the pinnacle of the positive mitzvah to give *tzedakah*, is based upon the law which immediately follows, that one must not "take from him interest . . . I am the Lord your God."[7]

---

5. It is equally an offense for any party to play any role in this illicit transaction. See *Shulchan Aruch, Yoreh Deah* 160:1.

6. Lev. 25:35.

7. "Who took you out of Egypt." The juxtaposition of *tzedakah*, the prohibition against taking interest, and the Exodus from Egypt illustrates an intrinsic connection between the three. Therefore the Siphra comments on this connection that whoever acknowledges the mitzvah of interest acknowledges the Exodus from Egypt. Conversely whoever denies the mitzvah of interest denies the Exodus from Egypt. It is somewhat strange that to appreciate the Rambam's highest level of *tzedakah*, it is necessary to analyze the Exodus from Egypt. This less than simple connection is discussed by the master of the "Simple Interpretation," Rashi, who explains that the prohibition on interest is connected with the tenth and final plague which occurred in Egypt, the slaughter of the Egyptian first-born. God is therefore telling the Jewish people that "just as I distinguished (among the Egyptians) between a first-born

The Siphra takes the words "I am the Lord your God," and suggests that "Whoever accepts the burden of the laws of interest, accepts [God and the] yoke of heaven." To lend money without interest, to forgo one's hard-earned wealth for the sake of a mitzvah, clearly displays one's faith in God. Consequently, some commentators[8] explain that when a Jew lends without interest, he displays his total lack of concern for personal profit from that money. He illustrates his faith in the Divine, and consequently accepts the yoke of heaven.

A LION'S SHARE OF THE WAGES

There is a famous story about a Jew living in the slums of New York in a state of great poverty, who was prepared to undertake any form of employment in order to feed his wife and family. Scouring newspapers and going from place to place in order to find a job, the Jew

---

and one who was not a first-born, I also distinguish and punish those who lend money to a Jew with interest and pretend that it [the money] belongs to a non-Jew" (*Bava Metziah* 61:6). Thus the lending of money to a Jew for interest appears to deny God's powers to distinguish.

However, this explanation is unsatisfactory for an understanding of the Rambam's highest level of *tzedakah*, since it relies on God's power of distinguishing only in the specific situation where a Jew demands interest from a fellow Jew, and pretends that the money he is lending is actually the money of a Gentile. However, if a Jew simply performs the sin of lending to a fellow Jew with interest (and does not pretend that the money he is using belongs to a Gentile), this does not appear to have any relationship whatsoever with the Exodus from Egypt.

8. See *Kli Yakar*, ibid.

was totally unable to find anything at all. However, one day as he was walking past the circus, he saw a sign outside advertising a job and so he decided to apply. Yet he was alarmed to learn that the circus's lion had recently died, and the advertised job involved dressing-up and pretending to be the lion. His utter desperation resulted in his application for the job, which he was successful in attaining.

The next day, the circus opened and the Jew found himself standing for hour after hour, dressed as a lion, and in a cage—next to a large growling bear. However, tedium soon turned to utter fright, when the Jew noticed that the door connecting his cage to the giant bear was actually ajar. Feeling no braver because of his ferocious lion's outfit, the Jew began to tremble uncontrollably, as the gigantic bear pushed open the connecting door, and advanced toward him; and although not religious, the Jew could think of nothing to do, but fall to the floor and scream the words of so many famous Jewish martyrs, "*Shema Yisroel, Hashem Elokeinu, Hashem Echod*" ("Hear O'Israel, the Lord our God is One").

To which the bear immediately responded in a Brooklyn accent "*Boruch Shem K'vod Malchuso Leolam Voed*" ("Blessed is His name, Whose kingdom is forever").

The famous *Shema* prayer which a Jew recites every morning and evening, and which countless martyrs have gone to their deaths with, proudly proclaiming the oneness of God, is the classic acceptance of the heavenly yoke. Such acceptance is a prerequisite for the performance of all mitzvahs.

However, Siphra's the connection between the laws of charity and an acceptance of the yoke of heaven appears somewhat superficial, since it fails to distinguish between "the yoke of heaven" and "trust in God." When a Jew recites the *Shema* prayer, he proudly proclaims his acceptance of the yoke of heaven. At this level, he will refrain from lending money with interest. However he will not necessarily lend without interest—he may simply refrain from lending completely. Therefore, by not lending at all, he is not rejecting the heavenly yoke (by lending with interest), but he is also not displaying his trust in God (by lending without interest). There is an important difference between acceptance of the yoke of heaven and trust in God, and so the Rambam's highest level of *tzedakah*, the interest-free loan, seems only explained as a "matter of trust."

DO WHAT I DO

When a Jew performs a mitzvah, he first recites a blessing which includes the words "God has sanctified us with *His* commandments." Therefore the mitzvahs which a Jew performs are known as "His [God's] commandments."

The Alter Rebbe explains that "*His* commandments" means that "He also performs them."[9] Therefore, with acceptance of the heavenly yoke as the preliminary to the performance of a mitzvah, a Jew can be inspired by the thought that God performs the "same" mitzvahs too.

While God performs mitzvahs before a Jew does[10] (in order to give the Jew the required strength and inspiration), there is a second stage to God's perfor-

---

9. *Likutei Torah, Deuteronomy* 9d; see also *Sefer HaMaamorim* 5710 (KPS, 1970), pp. 209ff.

10. It is also explained in the Midrash (*Shemos Rabbah* 30) that "What He does, He commands us to do," which means before a Jew undertakes any mitzvah (and even

mance of mitzvahs "that whenever a person studies Torah, God studies opposite him."[11] Thus, (i) inspired by the mitzvah of God, (ii) a Jew performs a mitzvah, which (iii) succeeds in inspiring God to perform that mitzvah once again. Hence, the motivation which the Jew derived by knowing God had performed the mitzvah first should be dramatically increased by the knowledge that his mitzvah is actually inspiring God to perform that same mitzvah again.[12] How could it be that God chose to allow the Jews' performance of mitzvahs to influence him to such a degree?

THE BIRTHDAY CAKE OF SHAME

Although a gift to *tzedakah*, which awards only benefit and no detriment to the beneficiary, would appear far more generous than an interest-free loan, this ignores the fact that it is the desire of human nature to achieve. The human psyche is predisposed to having an effect upon the world, to the point that the definition of being

---

before the prerequisite of accepting the Heavenly Yoke), the inspiration which he receives is based on the fact that God has already performed this mitzvah before him. See also Jerusalem Talmud, *Rosh Hashanah* 1:3.

11. Midrash (*Tanna d'vei Eliyahu Raba*, ch. 18).

12. Obviously, God does not require us to perform such mitzvahs for him to do likewise, moreover this forms part of His Divine desire to create a dwelling place down below, and thus the Divine choice was that a Jew should be inspired to perform God's will—which is achieved by God performing the mitzvah first; and also achieves the Divine performance of mitzvahs simultaneously with the performance of Jewish mitzvahs.

alive "is to achieve—to have an effect."[13] The Jerusalem
Talmud[14] condemns a payment which is given without any effort or detriment on the part of the receiver
and awards it the epithet, "Bread of shame."[15]

---

13. The Talmud explains that "Jacob never died," and
the reason is that "While his seed is alive, he is alive." This
means that while one's descendants behave as if one is
alive, and one has an effect upon the world, then consequently one is truly alive.

14. Tractate *Orlah* 1:3.

15. The importance of achieving and making one's
own way within the world is illustrated by the concept of
a birthday. At first glance, birth is not a cause for celebration for the individual who has entered into the world: to
the extent that while he remains in the womb, the Talmud
explains that "he is taught and understands the entire
Torah [Nidah 30b]." However, upon emergence into the
world, an angel smacks him on the lip and the entire Torah
is forgotten; He is then obligated to spend the whole of his
life devoted to acquiring a small fraction of the Torah which
he once knew. Therefore, a birth does not appear to be a
cause for joy or celebration, and it could even be conjectured
that the reason a baby cries at birth is because he has forgotten the entire Torah and realizes that he will never again
acquire even a percentage of the understanding he once had.

Yet, a birthday is a source for celebration, to the extent
that what one achieves by one's own hard work and dili-
gence is appreciated in a manner incomparable to that
which one acquires as a free gift. Therefore, the "free-gift
Torah" which one appreciated in the womb does not com-
pare in the satisfaction that it gives its owner to the "hard-
earned Torah" which he will learn throughout his life, even
though quantitatively this awareness of Torah will be far
weaker. From a personal-achievement perspective, the
birth is of great importance, because the person will learn
the Torah by his own hard work, "by the sweat of his brow."

There is a story[16] of a wealthy landowner who hired a peasant to do work for him at a very high rate of pay. The only problem was that although the landowner asked the peasant to swing his sickle—an action which the peasant was expert in—the sickle was actually to be swung in the dining room of the landowner's house. The peasant would be paid a large sum of money, but he would achieve nothing. He would simply swing the sickle in mid-air, all day long.

Although the financial offer was one which he could not refuse, it did not take long before the peasant gave up the job in dismay, and begged to be relieved. The peasant explained that he had nothing to show for his efforts and that he could not continue performing a task which achieved nothing.

God arranged the world in such a way that the Jew's performance of a mitzvah is able to elicit a simultaneous (second) performance by God. There can be no more significant achievement for a Jew, than the fact that when he performs a mitzvah, this inspires God to do likewise. If God simply performed His mitzvah before that of the Jew, and did not perform afterwards, it would be the case that the Jew received his inspiration for free. It would be the "Bread of Shame," and the Jew may feel that his performance—like that of the "sickle-swinging peasant"—has achieved nothing tangible.

IMITATION—A HIGHER FORM OF FLATTERY

Chassidic philosophy asserts[17] that interest means "receiving profit for past glories." The lender receives a

---

16. *Sefer HaSichos* 5680–87 (KPS, 1992), p. 27.
17. *Likutei Sichos*, vol. 3, pp. 1007ff.

benefit, because the money that was lent once belonged to him, even though at present the money is the borrower's.

This is analogous to God performing a mitzvah before a Jew, and then deriving the benefit afterward—meaning a case of God "living on past glories," by failing to join the Jew in his performance of the mitzvah.

Consequently, lending money at interest would be an announcement to God that one is not interested in stage two—God performing mitzvahs as a partner.[18] The mitzvah of lending without interest is a beautiful illustration of the mechanics of a mitzvah, since just as God inspires at the beginning but refuses to live on "past glories" and plays a partnership role throughout our performance of mitzvahs, so too must the Jew, when he lends money to a fellow Jew, refuse to live on the original action alone. He should instead, become a partner.[19]

As "*tzedakah* weighs against all mitzvahs," so to does the "lending of money without interest," since both engender a feeling of having fulfilled all mitz-

---

18. The Midrash explains that a person who lends money without interest "is considered as if he has fulfilled all the mitzvahs" (*Shemos Rabbah* 31:4), due to the fact that the fulfilment of the mitzvah of lending without interest is analogous to God's active participation in our Divine service.

19. This is the concept of a *Heter Iska*, which allows a Jew to lend money to a fellow Jew not as a borrower but as a partner in the business. Therefore, when the borrower does business, he does so with the share belonging to the lender and the profit received by the lender is that which is earned by the money which still belongs to him. The *Heter Iska*, just like the performance of mitzvahs by God in conjunction with the Jew, is basically a "partnership clause."

vahs. When a Jew performs the mitzvah of lending money without interest, he has not only received his inspiration from God's mitzvah above, he also inspires God to do the same mitzvah at the same time.[20]

The achievement of a partnership with God illustrates the dynamic of the "interest-free" loan itself which is a partnership between the rich and the poor. Just as the Jew gets extra inspiration by the thought that his mitzvah is being mirrored above (that he is truly achieving, and that his deeds are having an effect), so too does the poor man feel a sense of pride when the money he receives is not the "Bread of Shame"—It is a partnership agreement, whereby he is able to achieve and have an effect, and where the wealthy man treats him as an equal.

This is clearly the highest level of *tzedakah* because it represents *Imitatio Dei* (Replicating the Divine). A Jew is giving *tzedakah*, just as God is giving *tzedakah*, in the manner of a partnership—he gives and receives and this inspires him to give (and give) again.

---

20. One can therefore appreciate the connection between (a) the prohibition of interest, (b) the Exodus from Egypt, and (c) the acceptance of the Yoke of Heaven. The prohibition on accepting interest illustrates the dynamics of a mitzvah and the interrelationship between the performance down below by a Jew and the performance of God above. Since this particular mitzvah is representative of all mitzvahs, and since it illustrates the importance of the Divine as the precursor to mitzvah-performance by a Jew, it is a clear expression of the acceptance of the Heavenly yoke. By establishing a connection with the Divine, a Jew connects to the infinite and is able to behave in an unlimited manner—able to break beyond all barriers. This bursting beyond limitations and boundaries is the spiritual corollary of the Exodus from Egypt (the word "Egypt," in Hebrew, is the same as the word for "boundaries").

14
Commanding Obedience

Alan Dershowitz, the prominent law professor and prolific author, has an "opinion" on everything. It is consequently not surprising that he has written on the subject of *tzedakah*, and particularly the gifts of irreligious Jews to religious institutions. In his excellent bestseller *Chutzpah*, Dershowitz writes that charitable donations to Chabad-Lubavitch "reflect the reality that the Lubavitch movement works very hard at getting Jews to return to their roots." However, he also suggests that such donations "reflect nostalgia for, and guilt over abandoning the 'old' ways . . . [as well as] . . . a sense that the Lubavitch way is the 'authentically' Jewish way, and that secular Jews are not authentic Jews."[1]

In reality, there are many Jewish "givers" who do not follow a lifestyle consistent with much of Jewish law, but nevertheless contribute large amounts of *tzedakah*, often exclusively to Jewish charities. Such a phenomena allows some to argue that a non-observant Jew who is

---

1. Alan Dershowitz, *Chutzpah* (New York: Little, Brown & Co., 1991), p. 335.

somewhat indifferent to the existence of God could not really be described as having performed a mitzvah in the "authentically Jewish way" when he gives to *tzedakah*, since he is not a firm believer in the philosophical tenets that are demanded by his religion. Consequently, his donation could be seen as a "good deed" rather than a mitzvah. Since *tzedakah* is a commandment from God, to what extent can it be said that a "non-observant" or "non-believing" Jew performs an "authentic" mitzvah when he donates money to charity?

One is inclined to argue that a Jew, whatever his background, has a claim to "equal rights," that he can undertake the act of giving charity and the fact that he is performing a mitzvah should never be taken away from him. Moreover, the donations of a Jew who observes few of the requirements of Jewish law are in a way even more impressive, when it is considered that his desire to take part in Jewish activities still exists, despite the ease with which he could neglect Judaism completely.

From a mystical perspective, every Jew is seen as possessing a subconscious desire to perform the entire Torah,[2] and so "religious observance" is seen as the extent to which this desire has reached a conscious state.[3] The mystic would argue that, in essence, he sees no difference between an "observant" and a "non-observant" Jew, a "believer" and a "non-believer," and while he is a vehement supporter of performing mitzvahs, the mystic would not discriminate between the validity of any Jew's donation to charity. Nevertheless, while this a Torah viewpoint, it is necessary to find support for this attitude from less esoteric sources.

---

2. Rambam, *Hilchos Girushin* 2:20—see also chapter 9, above.

3. See Tanya (*Likutei Amarim*), ch. 18–19.

Surely, throughout all the discussion in Jewish academic literature, it must be clearly stated how essential is belief as a component of each mitzvah. The mitzvah of *tzedakah* is plainly an act based on a belief in God, so exactly what does it mean, when the act is done, and the belief is absent?

A BADLY-BEHAVED FISH

The role of *belief* is discussed at great length by the Abarbanel (Rabbi Yitzchak Ben Yehudah, 1437–1508), who protested that the very first commandment incumbent upon every single person which is the mitzvah "to believe in God," is a contradiction in terms. Since the very idea of a mitzvah is a commandment from God Himself, it makes no sense to have a separate mitzvah of belief, as one must already believe before considering whether to perform any commandment.[4] The prerequisite of all mitzvahs is a belief in God, and so what purpose does a specific mitzvah to believe serve?

There was a Jew who was in such desperate need of money that when a group of missionaries knocked upon his door and offered $10,000 if he converted to their sect, he accepted immediately.

The only condition that the Jew was forced to accept was that he refrain from eating meat on Fridays, and having been offered such a vast sum of money, this "small" sacrifice seemed insignificant. The leader of the group subsequently opened his leather briefcase, produced a small bottle and walked toward the Jew.

"You have nothing to fear," said the leader, "I'm simply going to sprinkle a few drops of this holy water

---

4. *Sefer Rosh Emunah*, ch. 4.

on your head and you will no longer be a Jew, and you will instantly become a member of our group."

For the next few days "the Jew's" extravagance knew no bounds, he lavished gifts on his family and friends and was not in the least concerned by the culinary condition which accompanied this large sum of money. However, on the first Friday evening, while the Jew and his family were dining on a feast of hot meat, there was a sudden knock on the door; and standing behind was the head missionary.

"There is a rather strong aroma of meat in the air," he remarked accusingly, "I trust that it is not coming from your house."

"Of course not," replied the Jew.

Dissatisfied with this answer, the missionary burst into the room and was shocked to see the Jew's entire family devouring large platters of meat.

"Would you like to join us in this feast of fish?" enquired the Jew, with a smile on his face.

"I'm not stupid," replied the Missionary. "You have broken our condition, and this is obviously meat."

"Actually," replied the Jew, "this is fish. You see, this morning when I placed a pot of meat in the oven, I simply sprinkled a few drops of holy water on its head and informed it that no longer was it a piece of meat, but now it was a fish."

However much force an individual has at his disposal, he cannot command the absolute obedience of another. The missionary had failed from the very outset, since this particular Jew never had any intention of conceding to the requests and abstaining from meat. Obedience is a necessary prerequisite for any command, since if a person refuses to listen to anyone's directives, if his conviction is strong, nothing will persuade him otherwise. An example of this is the war hero who refuses to relinquish secrets to the enemy despite brutal torture. Thus a person has total free will, and effectively there is nobody, not even (so to speak) God Himself, who can force him to follow a command, if the person does not wish to do so.[5]

A favorite question of television talk-show hosts to their guests is, "If a powerful genie were to offer you one wish, what would you choose?" Occasionally, a "smart" guest retorts that his one wish would be to have a large number of further wishes. Such a reply is usually the source of much annoyance to the host and most of his audience, as it is predicated on foolishness. The question "you may have one wish" means that "I am willing to obey you, but just once": this statement itself limits the extent of the obedience and so the "smart" guest was clearly requesting something which was not on offer.

Obedience is a faculty which comes entirely from within and cannot be commanded, because the very definition of obedience is the willingness to be commanded. What use then, is a commandment which states, "Please, obey me!"

Consequently, the first commandment to believe in God, which requires "obeying His command," seems to be backwards logic. A mitzvah is a commandment, which by its very definition presumes the obedience of its follower. Not only is it necessary to believe in God before even considering whether or not to perform one of His mitzvahs, but this belief must be accompanied by a willingness to carry out His instruction. How could it be then, that after a person has found faith in God, and time for the "Divine Plan," the first thing that he

---

5. Nevertheless, this state of affairs was created and is sustained at God's will.

is commanded to do is to acquire the selfsame belief
which he has already attained.

"THOU SHALT KNOW!"

There is a story of a young Jewish boy,[6] living in the
Ukraine in the eighteenth Century, who returned home
after a five-year stay in a *yeshiva* (academy of Jewish
learning). His father was eager to discover the great
wisdom that his son had accumulated from all his Talmudic study.

"Nu," inquired the father, "what is the most profound thing which you learned during your time in
yeshivah?"

"I learned that God exists," the son proudly replied.

However, after the great expense that the father had
incurred to finance his son's education, he was dis-
gusted at the meager nature of his son's reply, and to
prove his point, he immediately summoned his maid.

"Do you believe that God exists?" inquired the
father.

"Of course I do," replied the maid without a moment's hesitation.

"You see," the father pronounced turning to his
son, "even our simple maid believes that God exists;
and you took five years to find out."

"She may *believe* that He exists," replied the son,
"but I *know*."

Since there appears to be an advantage of knowledge over plain faith, the Abarbanel accordingly explains the first mitzvah as "A Commandment of Knowl-

---

6. Believed to be the young R. Levi Yitzchak of Berdit-
chev (1740–1810).

edge," rather than one of belief. He clarifies that there are certain philosophical truths that a Jew must know about his Creator: (a) That God is totally independent; (b) That God encompasses all of existence, etc.—and this forms the basis of the first mitzvah, the commandment "to *know* God."[7]

According to this explanation, there is a perfectly reasonable path in the service of God. Firstly, a person has to believe in God; and only after this is he ready to begin fulfilling God's commands, the first of which is "to know Him"—to understand the nature of God, and, armed with this knowledge, to then venture to perform the other mitzvahs. The Abarbanel has thus clarified that the first mitzvah is not "to believe in God," which is a totally pre-mitzvah activity, but rather "to know Him."[8]

HE WHO MUST BE OBEYED

It would appear from the approach of the Abarbanel that, as far as God is concerned, knowledge is more precious than belief. Quite simply, it is a mitzvah to know God, but there is no such command to believe in Him. When God gave the Torah at Mount Sinai, He did not instruct the Jews to believe in Him, but simply assumed that they already did. From this viewpoint, it appears that Judaism is more interested in philosophical truth and comprehensible logic than matters of faith and blind intuition. In fact, most *yeshivahs* around the world spend nearly the entire day learning Torah, but rarely ever discuss belief in God.

---

7. *Derech Mitzvosecha* of the Tzemach Tzedek, *Haamonus Elokus* 45a.

8. *Sefer Rosh Emunah*, ibid.

However, if Judaism is reduced to mere intellectual discussion, however profound or ingenious, then it has become an academic "subject" and not "the way of life" which it has been for hundreds of generations. The fact that a Jew believes in God is the source and reason for all his Torah learning and all his mitzvah observance.[9] Without this faith, he would not find the motivation to perform any of the 613 commandments, or learn even one page of the Talmud, since, as the Abarbanel notes, a "feeling of willingness and obedience must precede the observance of all mitzvahs."

Consequently, the fact that "belief" could not form part of the first mitzvah should not cause a person to lose respect for the concept of simple faith. In reality one is not commanded to believe, simply because belief is so lofty and so profound that it cannot be commanded.[10]

Countless stories are told of Jews who have little or no connection with observant Jewish life, but nevertheless have a Jewish identity which is so strong that they would die for it. Many people who quite frankly confess that they really do not "know" if they believe

---

9. *Likutei Sichos*, vol. 27 (KPS, 1989), p. 251

10. The Talmud compares this quality of "belief as the will to obey" to the placing of the yoke of an ox around its neck, which harnesses the power of the ox, leading it to perform the tasks which its master requires. In a similar way, a Jew has to accept the "Yoke of Heaven" before the performance of any mitzvah. In effect, this acceptance and willingness to obey includes within it every single mitzvah which the person will perform, since such acceptance is their ultimate cause. The faculty of "accepting the Yoke of Heaven," being that it is so primary, is deeply rooted in the psyche of the Jew, and is considered to come from the essence of the soul.

in God, actually spend an enormous part of their time involved in Jewish charities, causes, and activities. Yet if one understands that every Jew innately "believes" in God, then it is obvious why all of these activities are undertaken. It is often the case that, despite the Jew's inner belief, he has not yet learned enough philosophical truths to be thoroughly satisfied with a "knowledge of God." So, just because a Jew does not fulfil the intellectually demanding mitzvah of "knowing God," does not mean he does not "believe" in God. The very fact that he has such a strong desire to remain Jewish shows that he is willing to obey, while not yet appreciating all the rules.

The Polish *yeshivah* student may have returned home, proud that he had spent many years devoting his mind to the study of Torah, fulfilling the will of God; but his father taught him an important lesson. All the Torah learning he had acquired, and all the mitzvahs he had performed, did not make him any more Jewish than the simple maid. Both he and she believed in God, and the only difference between them was that the son's belief had led him to discover how to use his mind and body to serve God. Nevertheless, his father reminded him that this great wisdom he had acquired was merely "a consequence of his belief," and had not superseded it.

Spending five years in *yeshivah* made the boy discover what it meant to be Jewish, but he himself did not become any more Jewish in the process, so in essence he is no different from the maid.

CHARITY WITHOUT KNOWING

It is readily observable that most Jewish survivors of the Holocaust have very strong "opinions" concerning God.

To understand and "know" God after the events that they have witnessed is almost beyond the realms of human ability, and yet a remarkable number of survivors remain orthodox and observant. Even amongst those who *know* that they can no longer understand God, and claim not to believe in Him, there are some wonderful stories of belief.

Throughout the Rabbi's entire sermon, there was one old man who continually heckled. Unmoved by the sincerity of the words, and becoming increasingly annoyed by the Rabbi's obvious faith in the goodness of God, the old man became louder and more abusive with his criticism. After the Rabbi had concluded his oration, the man approached him, absolutely overcome with anger.

"How can you make such a speech," said the old man, "when God sat by and watched while six million of our people were slaughtered. I cannot accept God after the horrors that I witnessed, and refuse to apologize, Rabbi, for the fact that, after Auschwitz, I do not believe in Him."

As the man became more angry, the synagogue service was drawing to a conclusion, and finally reached the *Kaddish* prayer for mourners.

"How could He have not intervened," the old man continued, "Belief in God now would be a . . . Oh, excuse me Rabbi, *Yisgadal, Veyiskadash S'hmei Rabbo* . . ."[11]

A Jew can quite understandably have lost the strength to perform the mitzvah of knowing God. He has seen so much that he can no longer understand or accept the "philosophical truths" about God, but he still *believes* in Him and wants to perform mitzvahs

---

11. The opening words of the mourners' prayer which declare the "greatness" and "holiness" of God.

such as the reciting of *Kaddish*. The reason for this is that "to know God" is only one of 613 commands, but *belief* in God, which is innate to every Jew, is the basis of all 613 commands. If one does not perform certain mitzvahs, for whatever reason, even if it is the first mitzvah—the knowledge of God Himself—one is still totally Jewish and his belief is still intact.

If a Jew gives to *tzedakah*, he fulfils a mitzvah of the Torah in the "authentically Jewish way." His desire to do so stems from the fact that he is "authentically Jewish"—he innately believes in God, and he consequently wants to perform His will. Whether or not this individual also performs the mitzvah of knowing God and is convinced of His existence does not in any way affect the validity or authenticity of his *tzedakah*, because "knowledge of God" and "giving *tzedakah*" are totally separate mitzvahs. Many Jews who give large amounts to charity would confess that they "don't know" if they believe, and yet these large donations, almost exclusively to Jewish charities, demonstrate the Jews' true inner belief. Whether or not a Jew "knows" God does not affect the fact that he is completely Jewish, that he is a genuine believer, and thus he is able to fulfil the mitzvah of *tzedakah* in the most "authentic" possible manner.

15
A Reward by Any Other Name Would Be as Sweet

The principal conductor of the London Symphony Orchestra, Michael Tilson-Thomas, in his book *Viva Voce*, describes the time that he "introduced *Yiddishkeit* into Bali."[1] The Jewish conductor was staying in a small village outside Ubud and spent several days teaching the villagers Western music. Using his little Yamaha synthesizer, he decided that he would play something special for them.

"While they listened attentively I could tell that none of the Bach, Mozart, Gershwin, or Beatles tunes made any impression on them. Then one day I hit on playing one of my favorite Hassidic tunes. This little Jewish tune, with all its resigned sing-song cadences, they took to immediately. They asked me to play it again and again. I could still hear them singing it as

---

1. Michael Tilson-Thomas, *Viva Voce* (London: Faber and Faber, 1984) p. 207.

they disappeared along the trail into the bamboo
jungle."

Judaism exudes spirituality, a fact that is particularly expressed within the Chassidic approach to being
Jewish. Jews are spiritual people, and are constantly
aspiring to appreciate the lofty and the sublime. Ultimately, a Jew does mitzvahs because he is a spiritual
being.[2] Yet throughout Jewish sources, a multitude of
rewards are proffered for the fulfilment of mitzvahs,
particularly the giving of tzedakah. In the Talmud[3] one
is actually told he will become rich if he is scrupulous
with charitable gifts, and God specifically and unpre-
cedentedly challenges a Jew to "Please test Me, through
[giving to tzedakah] and [see] if I will pour upon you
blessings without limit."[4]

Many sections of the Torah deal with the subject
of rewards, particularly the portion of Bechukosai ("My
Statutes"),[5] which enumerates at great length the pro-
spective fortunes or losses which will ensue as a consequence of mitzvah observance. The Abarbanel (amongst
others) finds great difficulty with this entire passage,
because although it is an accepted principle that reward and punishment exist within Judaism, it appears strange that the vast majority of rewards with
which the Torah tempts its followers are physical and
materialistic.

---

2. Furthermore, even the *physical* energy of a Jew is
considered to come directly from his Godly soul, even
though it is manifested through the animal soul. See Tanya,
Iggeres HaTeshuvah, ch. 6; *Kuntres Umayon*, ch. 7; *Likutei
Sichos* vol. 4, 6th ed. (KPS, 1992), p. 1206.

3. *Taanis* 9a.

4. See *Shulchan Aruch, Yorah Deah*, 247:10, *Rema*—"It is
forbidden to test God with any [mitzvah] other than this."

5. *Vayikra* 26:4 and on.

Surely, those accustomed to following the Torah are of a spiritual and religious disposition, and it would seem more appropriate to give more specific coverage to the spiritual rewards of the "Next World." From a superficial survey of the Five Books of Moses, it appears that not only does Judaism overemphasize the subject of rewards, but it is mainly interested in tangible rewards of a physical nature. This would seem to present a disappointment to more spiritually-inclined people, who would rather perform mitzvahs for heaven's sake.[6]

---

6. The Kli Yakar (R. Shlomo Ephraim ben Aaron of Lunschitz, 1550–1619) reconciles the apparent overemphasis on the physical aspect of reward (on the basis of a law codified by the Rambam, *Mishneh Torah, Hilchos Teshuvah* 9:1). He explains that all the material wealth that is offered within the Torah is not intended as any sort of substantive reward, since it is a well known fact that the principal reward in Judaism is offered in the World to Come. What is mentioned is that if a Jew earnestly performs mitzvahs, God will reciprocate by providing him with the appropriate "working conditions" in which to carry out more mitzvahs. Thus, God promises that giving *tzedakah* will not diminish one's personal wealth, and so the physical bounty which is offered by the Torah is not really a reward, but rather part of a contract from the Creator. This Divine contractual promise declares that if a Jew actively performs mitzvahs, God will make it easier for him to continue to do so. In this vein the material wealth offered by the Torah is seen to be more along the lines of small perks which make life easier, rather than real potential earnings.

However, a vast number of respected commentators on the Torah state that when physical, tangible bounty is offered as a consequence of mitzvah fulfilment, it is genuine earnings from doing God's will. This theory of physical rewards as "mere working condition" is not universally accepted.

A QUESTION OF ETHICS

One of the most famous statements made in *Avos* ("Ethics")[7] is that a person should not serve God for the sake of a reward, but that the correct way to be is "like a person who serves his master, not to receive a reward."[8] A Jew should be the type of servant whose love for his master is so profound that his service is not guerdon-provoked. Is this advice of our sages in *Ethics* not a clear contradiction to the vast collection of temptations in the Torah?[9] Particularly in relation to *tzedakah*, the Talmudic promise of wealth if one donates money to charity must surely inspire a form of service which is for the sake of the reward of riches. Why does the Torah specifically offer rewards for giving *tzedakah* and performing other mitzvahs, and at the same time

---

7. *Ethics of the Fathers*. Amongst the entirety of Jewish Literature, this collection of saying of the sages of the Talmudic period is considered to be one of the most informative and resourceful guides to the ethical behavior of the Jew. It lists a miscellany of guidance, concerning life in general, serving God in particular, and the general attitude that a Jew has to have in approaching his position within the world.

8. Ch. 1, Mishnah 3.

9. One may be tempted to answer that *Avos* is only an ethical work, that it deals with ideals, pleasant behavior, as it's referred to in Hebrew as *"milei d'chassidus"* (examples of pious conduct), but it does not really describe a real and practical approach to Judaism. It merely portrays a picture of ideal behavior. Yet, *Avos* is not a pleasant addition to the Torah, but rather a guide as to that which the Torah actually wants, conduct which may not be so obvious from a simple reading of verses in the Torah. Therefore, when a Jew reads it, he should not see *Avos* as an ethical ideal, but as a moral obligation.

clearly demand that a Jew serve God for no ulterior motive?

One answer to this question is found in the *Hilchos Teshuvah* ("Laws of Repentance") of the Rambam. In this section of laws, the Rambam discusses the ideal mentioned in *Avos* concerning serving God "not for the sake of receiving a reward." He comments that "this quality is a very great one indeed, and certainly not every person merits to reach this level." Therefore to serve God without reward in mind is deemed a lofty achievement, and the beginning of one's Divine service is expected to be accompanied by some thought of reward.

This is consistent with the Rambam's philosophy in his *Guide for the Perplexed*, where he writes that Torah (and the rewards in *Bechukosai*) "speaks to the majority;"[10] therefore exciting physical rewards are offered for mitzvahs, since "the Majority" seem to require this type of inspiration.[11] Revelations of Godliness,

---

10. Maimonides, *Moreh Nevuchim*, part 3, ch. 34. The Rambam brings a Talmudic proof (Tractate *Pesachim* 50b) which states "a person should always be occupied in Torah and mitzvahs, even though he does not do so altruistically." The Rambam concludes from this statement that a person should teach all types of Jews (even small children or highly ignorant individuals) to serve God, even in order to receive a reward, because they will "eventually come to appreciate this form of Divine service [for its own sake]."

11. This explanation also makes clear Tractate *Kesubbos* 111b, which discusses many physical rewards concerning Messianic times. The same difficulty arises with these sections, that why is an era which is so spiritual and holy as the times of redemption, filled with physical reward?

The answer is that the world is not interested in lofty spiritual revelations and total occupation and immersion

and rewards in the world to come, may not excite the average Jew into mitzvah-observance, yet great wealth, health, and happiness as rewards certainly will. The Torah appears to be advocating rewards for the sake of pragmatism, as an admission that without recompense "a majority" would not be fulfilling mitzvahs.

WOULDN'T YOU EXPECT A LITTLE MORE FROM GOD?

The Lubavitcher Rebbe is a strong proponent of the universality of Torah, and has always stressed that the Torah is applicable "at all times, in all places, and *for all people.*"[12] Therefore to proclaim that *Bechukosai* is exclusively speaking to "the majority"—those on a lower spiritual level—is problematic. If one already serves God on a "high level" and does not require any

---

in Torah: therefore our Sages had to tell us the bottom line, that when the Messiah comes the physical world will enjoy an abundance of physical fancies. Therefore, if one does not want redemption for the "new appreciation of Torah" which will be available, one can be excited and inspired by the innovations in physicality which will be on offer.

12. In fact, Rabbi Aryeh Kaplan z"l mentions in his introduction to his modern translation of the Bible (*The Living Torah* [Moznaim, 1981]) that it is an insult to translate the Torah in archaic language, since one who does the disastrous job of making the Torah look old-fashioned denigrates the very essence of what Torah is: an eternal communication between God and man. Would one not hope that the words with which God chose to speak to us would not become obsolete? God's words are eternally significant, so to translate the Torah and make it sound like an antiquated document is an insult to the Torah, and it is a grave sin.

reward as an incentive, what does this section of the "universally-applicable" Torah mean for such an individual?[13]

A TRAVELLING REPAIRMAN

There was once a Chassid who toured the United States strengthening Jewish awareness in small communities. When questioned as to what exactly was his trade, he replied that he was in the business of mending Torah Scrolls; and proceeded to explain that since every Jew is "like a letter in the Torah, my job is to re-write those which have become erased."

Upon returning to his Rebbe, the Chassid was rebuked for his use of this analogy. The Rebbe explained that a more accurate analogy would be that of an engraver. He had to find an engraved tablet of stone in which the letters had become filled with dirt; and the Chassid's job was merely to blow that dirt away, to reveal the letters which had always been there.

---

13. See *Likutei Sichos, Bechukosai* 5751. Furthermore, the problem with learning that *Bechukosai* is principally for the lowly, specifically contradicts a fundamental explanation on the meaning of this very section. The *Toras Cohanim* states that the words "If you will follow 'My Statutes' (*Bechukosai*) . . . and perform them," means one has "to toil in Torah."

When our Sages instruct "toiling" in Jewish law and total immersion in Torah, they demand that every fiber of a person's being be preoccupied and devoted to study and mitzvah observance. Consequently, *Bechukosai* is one of the most lofty and sublime lessons to every Jew: that to serve God means 100% devotion.

The uniqueness of engraved letters is that they are not superimposed and added to the medium on which they are written (like ink on paper), but rather they are carved out, which means that they are totally one entity with the substance on which they are written. Chassidic philosophy explains that the world *Bechukosai* (which literally means "my statutes") is etymologically related to the word *chakika*, meaning "engraved."[14] *Bechukosai* means a Jew must not soak up, absorb, or become covered by Torah; he must become *engraved* by it.

DON'T BE JEWISH, BE A JEW

A Jew has to serve God with his being and not merely with his mind or body. It must not merely be the case that Judaism is the most exciting thing in one's life, and it is not sufficient to be obsessed with Torah.[15] There has to be a process of metamorphosis from a human being to a Torah being, and the source for this most sublime level of Divine Service is the section on rewards in *Bechukosai*. If it were not explicit in the Torah, that rewards will affect the mundane things in life, one could fallaciously presume that when it comes down to the mundane, being Jewish is not a fundamental.

---

14. *Likutei Torah*, loc cit. *Likutei Sichos*, vol. 3, p. 1013; vol. 4, p. 1056; *Sefer HaMaamorim* 5665, p. 224.

15. Hence, the Torah states concerning itself "It is your *life*, and the length of your days" (Deut. 30:20), signifying that the Torah should become the totality of one's life [see *Avodah Zorah* 3b; *Zohar* II 42a, 278b). For this reason, this quote was included within the daily evening service (see *Berachos* 68b).

"Judaism is about spirituality, it's about religious activity, and holy things, but when it comes down to the most mundane, the most simple things, why does that have anything to do with being Jewish? When I eat my supper, when I get the train to work, when I blow my nose, how can I be Jewish? What has that got to do with Judaism?" Of course, if a person is a Jew in his very being, in his essence, then everything he does is related to Judaism: he is a living Torah. The fact that when one walks to work, reads a book, or gives money to charity, he has to be Jewish, is only possible if one is engraved with Judaism.

The evidence that when one is involved in the most earthly of activities one still has to be Jewish is found in the Torah's emphasis on earthly rewards. Judaism accentuates reward, not only to incite toward observance: the Torah teaches us about mundane reward to teach us that we have to serve God also with mundane activity. Since reward is "measure for measure" (*midda c'neged midda*), whatever form the reward takes, that is the form which the Divine service which preceded must take.

Bechukosai illustrates the highest level of Divine service, since "toiling in Torah" and being "engraved with Torah" means that even when one is being mundane, he does it in a way that is Jewish. He does it in a manner of total submission to God, even when he is doing something that appears insignificant in the Divine Plan.[16]

The Talmud[17] states that in the Messianic era, "fruits will ripen in an instant, and all physical delights will be available like dust." The answer as to how the

---

16. See *Likutei Sichos* 5751, ibid.
17. *Kesubos* 111b.

Torah could tempt with such coarse and mundane things is that it is not intended as a temptation; it is an expression of the perfection of the world in Messianic times. The fact that fruits ripen instantly, is not supposed to tempt us to want the Messiah because we want quick fruit, but rather it expresses how perfectly the physical world will be united with God, since today's problems are only a result of the fact that "God's will" is not expressed in the physical world. Also, if a person decides that he does not want the Messiah to come, God forbid, because he may lose out in the physical, he has to know that not only will the physical be abundant in the future, but furthermore the true power of physicality is only going to be appreciated at this time. Since it says that "from my flesh I will perceive Godliness,"[18] it is clear that the future will be a time when God and the world will not be contradictions in terms, because the physical will no longer be an obstacle to the spiritual; as the very essence of God will be revealed in the world.

Since "tzedakah is equated to all the mitzvahs,"[19] it is clear that the manner and the giving of tzedakah has to set a precedent for the observance of all other mitzvots. If tzedakah is given for selfish motives, to achieve certain goals or to attain a reward, then a Jew's entire Divine service could be tarnished. Judaism stresses physical rewards because one has to be

---

18. Job 19:26. See also *Likutei Dibburim* II, pp. 332b ff, which relates the story of the great Chassid, Reb Hillel Paritcher, who said that when he learned the Chassidic explanation of this verse, that "his body was a *shpectiva*, a magnifying glass through which one can see Godhood, then the body (which was previously despicable to him) assumed significance for me."

19. *Bava Basra* 9a.

immersed in Divine service to the extent that he is *engraved* by it. Therefore, one should not give *tzedakah* to relieve a conscience, or to gain a reward, or even because one enjoys performing mitzvahs—*tzedakah* has to be given, simply, because a Jew has to give *tzedakah*.

A Jew has to proudly proclaim, "I'm Jewish, therefore I give." There need not be any intermediate processing, any contemplation, or even any learning to achieve this goal. If the Torah had not offered physical rewards for *tzedakah*, one may not think to give *tzedakah* in the most simple, physical way: just handing over the coin because one is Jewish.

16
An End to the Giving of Charity?

Having offered his profound sympathy on the bank-
ruptcy of a company in which his son had invested
heavily, the Rabbi was astonished to learn that the son
had successfully sold all his shares only one day before
the liquidation.

"How were you able to foresee that such a seemingly profitable company would face such problems,"
inquired the Rabbi.

"I was sitting in Synagogue, next to the Chairman
of the Company," responded the son, "and as I over-
heard his prayers, his yearning for the Messiah was so
intense, and his desire for the Redemption was so
strong, that I knew his business had to be in trouble."

The belief, for noble or ignoble motives, in a Messianic future—in a time when God's sovereignty will
be recognized by all nations—is a central theme within
Judaism. It is alluded to within the Bible, ubiquitous
in the Prophetic writings, and forms the core of our

daily prayers. However, as to whether many Jews really yearn for such a time is not so certain. The average Jew does not perceive that there is anything fundamentally wrong with his life, and has arrived at a comfortable accommodation with the society around him. Although Judaism is predicated on the hope of a better tomorrow. It was far easier to keep this idea alive in hard times, and it is profoundly difficult to do so today. However, are our lives really as satisfying as they may appear?

L'CHAIM, TO LIGHT!

A lightbulb is one of the most impressive inventions in the world. Unlike the use of candles, there is very little risk of fire, the light which it provides is far brighter, and it is operated at a "flick" of a switch. The lightbulb revolutionized life, and transformed the whole period of night and darkness into one that can be enjoyed as if it were day. While convenient and cheap to run, it offers a large amount of light in convenient and pleasant form.

However, only two percent of the electricity which a lightbulb receives is actually converted to light. The remainder of the electricity is totally wasted, and is dissipated as heat. Consequently, one should indeed be embarrassed to use a lightbulb, since the fact that it gives out a lot of light and is convenient to use is merely superficial, and the truth is that a lightbulb is highly inefficient and does its job poorly.

The principal problem is that the world has learned to live with this deficiency, and totally accept it. Most people are blissfully ignorant of the fact that a light bulb wastes the vast majority of the energy that it is given; and quite happily "flick" the switch twenty-four hours a day without considering the ridiculous amount of energy that is being squandered.

Ever since the destruction of the Second Temple, the Jewish people have been in exile, in body and in mind. "Exile" means that the world is acting inefficiently, and only a tiny fraction of the world's true ability to satisfy its inhabitants and its Creator is utilized. There is more than enough food to feed all the people in the world, and yet many are starving. However, the most saddening aspect of exile is the "exile mentality,"[1] whereby most people are generally contented with the standard of world civilization, accepting the world in a superficial way, like the convenience of a lightbulb: enjoying its convenience, while remaining apathetic to a total waste of resources.

FINDING THE REDEEMING FEATURE

There is a classic pronouncement in the Talmud that states, "How great is *Tzedakah*, that it brings close the Redemption."[2] Naturally, every aspect of Torah and mitzvahs has some sort of connection with bringing

---

1. See *Sefer HaSichos* 5751, vol.2 (KPS, 1992), p. 474, where the Rebbe explains, "What more can I do to make the Jewish people complain [to God] and cry out with sincerity, so as to achieve the actual coming of *Moshiach*. Everything that was done until now was insufficient, as is evidenced by the fact that we are still in exile; and most significantly, in an *'exile mentality'* concerning our relationship with God." It is further noted there that "In order to accelerate this further, myself, I will give to every one of you money to give to *tzedakah*."

2. *Bava Basra* 10a.

the Redemption,[3] yet this explicit reference asserts that *tzedakah* has a more powerful connection than other mitzvahs. The fact the Talmud singled out *tzedakah*, was not merely as an incentive to give, but rather an illustration that *tzedakah* has a more special connection with the Redemption of the world than any other mitzvah.

The Talmud[4] states that the difference between kindness and *tzedakah* is that kindness can be offered to either rich or poor people, however *tzedakah* can only be performed with the poor. Consequently, *tzedakah* as a gift to the poor means taking an existing person who is incapable of living through poverty, and bestowing upon him the means with which he can live a normal life.[5]

A true appreciation of *tzedakah* is the *metamorphosis* of a poor, inefficient individual into an efficient and productive one. So, the interdependence of *tzedakah* and Redemption is based on the fact that Redemption does not require rejection of the existing world and its replacement with a better one. "Redemption" is to improve the pre-existing world and to reveal its hidden potential, rather like making use of the other

---

3. The Rambam states that a belief in the Messiah and Redemption is one of the thirteen principles of the faith, and anyone who denies this, it is as if he denies the entire Torah. See Tanya, ch. 37: "The culmination of all our activity throughout the entire period of exile is the Messianic Era," and ch. 37 continues by specifically emphasizing the role of *tzedakah*.

4. *Succah* 49b.

5. This may be another reason why the Rambam considers the highest level of *tzedakah* to be supporting another person to the extent that they are able to become self sufficient.

ninety-eight percent of a lightbulb. Since "exile" ensures a sense of satisfaction with the inefficiencies of the world, Redemption means to make the world a totally efficient and productive place.[6] "*Tzedakah* brings close the Redemption," because charity to the poor—as the actualization of all the undiscovered potential within another human being—illustrates the same achievement as Redemption.

KING DAVID'S BROKEN SUCCAH

Tzedakah is not simply one means to bring about the redemption. The Talmud goes as far as to assert that "The Jews will be redeemed, *only* through *tzedakah.*"[7] The Alter Rebbe discusses this declaration in the *Tanya*[8] and writes, "The main object of observance these days

---

6. In Hebrew, the word *Golah*, which means exile, and the word *Geulah*, which means redemption, are spelt identically except for one letter, that is the additional *Aleph* in *Geulah*, redemption. At first glance, it is somewhat surprising that *Golah*, which signifies poverty, starvation, death, and the absence of revealed Godliness, has any connection to *Geulah*, which signifies peace, kindness, wealth, and the presence of God in the world. Since the name of something in Hebrew reflects its essence, it is evident that *Geula* is not a replacement for *Golah*—a process of destroying the world and replacing it with a superior one—but rather a display of the inherent potential and greatness of the existing world, and this is the significance of the additional letter *aleph* (which in Hebrew means 'one'): The revelation of God's unity *within* the world in order to perfect it, not via destruction or replacement.

7. Tractates *Shabbos* 139a and *Sanhedrin* 98a.

8. Igeres *Kodesh*, ch. 9.

which are immediately prior to the coming of the Messiah is the giving of *tzedakah*."

There are a series of questions and difficulties with this view, based upon the famous saying of the Sages "that the learning of Torah is equivalent to all other mitzvahs (even *tzedakah*),"[9]: but the Alter Rebbe dismisses this quite simply "as only applicable in their days." In Talmudic times, the learning of Torah was on a lofty and sublime level, and Jewish Law was learned with great depth and profound understanding. However, nowadays[10] the "principal service" is the giving of *tzedakah*, rather than the learning of Torah.[11]

The Alter Rebbe argues that in the later generations the presence of God on earth is so weak that it is necessary to do practical mitzvahs. God's presence within the world has "fallen to the [Kabbalistic] level of 'action' . . . and the only way to unite with this level of Godliness is through a corresponding degree of action, namely the act of *tzedakah*."[12] By means of physical mitzvahs, the Alter Rebbe asserts that God's presence can be returned to the physical fabric of the world more effectively than the spiritual task of learning Godly wisdom.[13]

---

9. Mishnah *Peah* 1:1.

10. Which are described by the Talmud as the days of "the footsteps of the Messiah"—*Sotah* 49b.

11. *Zohar* II, 9a. In our times, "The *Succah* (hut) of King David has fallen to the lowest depths" a Kabbalistic term, mentioned in the Zohar, which represents God's presence on earth.

12. *Iggeres Kodesh*, ch. 9.

13. According to Rav Dustai, the son of Yanai, God's presence can be enjoyed, by even the smallest charitable donation. He declares in Tractate *Bava Basra* (10a) "Come, let us see how the ways of God, differ from the ways of flesh

REPAIRMAN

While this emphasis upon *tzedakah* may appear to rely upon non-legal sources, the Alter Rebbe's rejecting the accentuation of Torah learning as the "principal service" is based on a fundamental principle in Jewish law. The jurisprudence of a *Hazman Gramah* means that when a person has the opportunity to do a mitzvah, if the facts are such that if he does not perform it immediately the opportunity will be lost, then a person is legally obliged to stop learning Torah, in order to fulfil that mitzvah.[14]

Consequently, the era in which we are living is one of *Hazman Gramah*, an era when there is a timely task that needs to be fulfilled—bordering on a state of emergency—and the task is to bring the presence of God back to earth in a physical, tangible manner. Therefore, there is a legal basis[15] for the statement of the Alter Rebbe that the supreme mitzvah in our generation, which pushes away Torah learning from the "number one" spot in the "mitzvah parade" is the action-packed mitzvah of *tzedakah*.

---

and blood—If someone brings a gift to a mortal King, he cannot be certain that it will be accepted, and even if it is, he cannot be sure that he will be allowed into the King's presence. However, with God; if a person gives even the smallest coin to *tzedakah*, he enjoys the Divine presence—as it is written 'Through *tzedakah*, I will behold your face' (Ps. 17:15)."

14. See *Shulchan Aruch, Yoreh Deah*, 249:5; *Shulchan Aruch HaRav, Hilchos Talmud Torah* 4:3, which makes specific reference to *tzedakah*.

15. See *Sefer Hisvadiyus* 5742, vol. 4 (Kfar Chabad: Lahak Hanachos, 1983), p. 1954.

THE NULLIFICATION OF *TZEDAKAH*
IN THE FUTURE?

The German philosopher Immanuel Kant, in his *Critique of Pure Reason*[16] declared Science forever incapable of solving the three fundamental problems of metaphysics: God, freedom, and immortality. This means that Kant contended that physics can never determine if God exists, if we have free will, or if God will grant us immortal life.

The innovative physicist Frank J. Tipler disagrees. In his monumental 1994 book *The Physics of Immortality: Modern Cosmology, God and the Resurrection of the Dead*,[17] Tipler argues that the "Omega Point Theory" is a perfectly sound scientific proof for the Messianic era and its resurrection of the dead. Consequently, these key concepts in Judaism become accepted scientific concepts, but while Tipler boldly advocates immortality, he is silent as to science's description of the Messianic era: What will the world be like?

Although it is certain that giving *tzedakah* is a catalyst for a worldwide Redemption, it is less certain whether the mitzvah of *tzedakah* will continue in a "redeemed" world. It may have been presumed that since the Rambam states "all delights and delicacies will be found as dust, and all good, will be abundant,"[18] the need for sustaining the poor will be rendered redundant in the Messianic age. Thus, what is the significance of giving *tzedakah*, after the Messiah comes? Particularly, since many authorities seem to rule that

---

16. Kant—1950—p. 29 & 46.
17. Frank J. Tipler, Anchor Books: Doubleday, 1994.
18. *Mishneh Torah, Hilchos Melachim*, ch. 12.

the future will see the invalidation of mitzvahs,[19] i.e., Rav Yosef asserts that "Mitzvahs will be nullified in the future." Consequently, the mitzvah of *tzedakah* will apparently be "nullified," too.

However, any repeal of the mitzvah to give charity is rejected by the assertion of the Rambam that "Jewish Law is eternal."[20] So, in a redeemed world, will *tzedakah* be "nullified" or is it "eternal"?[21]

---

19. This opinion is based on the Talmud, in Tractate *Nidah* (61b) which states "a garment which contains forbidden fabric mixtures (wool and linen) . . . may be used to prepare a shroud for a dead person. Rav Yosef says that 'from this we can conclude that mitzvahs will be nullified in the future.'"

Tosafos explains the logic behind Rav Yosef's statement to the extent that when the deceased person arises from his grave, he will be wearing the shroud; thus, it is obvious that the prohibition of forbidden fabrics cannot apply at that particular time.

20. *Mishneh Torah*, end of *Hilchos Megillah*.

21. The question is answered by the Talmudic source for the resurrection in Tractate *Sanhedrin* (90b), where it states that the scriptural source for the resurrection is the verse ". . . and you shall give from it, the heave offering . . . to Aaron the priest." The Talmud consequently proves that since Aaron the priest was not alive at the time that the heave offering was given, and he never entered Israel so that it could be given to him, "Rather [we must conclude] that in the future he will be resurrected and [the Jews] will give him the offering then."

From this piece of Talmud, it is obvious that Jewish Law will not be nullified in the future, since the heave offering will be given to Aaron after the time of the resurrection. The Rambam appears well supported in his view that "Jewish Law is eternal."

IT'S NOT A COMMAND—IT'S A PLEASURE!

Ultimately, mitzvahs will be nullified, but this is only to the extent that one appreciates the word mitzvah [not according to the Chassidic explanation of a "connection to God"; but rather] according to the simple meaning of a mitzvah, which is as a commandment to a human being. In the future, a Jew will not be subject to any mitzvah as commandments, and consequently, our perception of *tzedakah* will ascend from its simple level of being a mitzvah (commandment) to the lofty heights of being a *"Jewish Law"* (which is the "will of God"[22]).

The Talmudic scholar was so engrossed in his books that he failed to notice that his entire yeshiva was on fire. As his colleagues screamed for his attention, he continued reading, oblivious to their desperation. Soon the flames reached him, and when he finally noticed, the scholar began to pray to God that he could continue learning, and not have to vacate the room.

---

22. On this basis, the seeming difficulties in the words of Rav Yochanan can be resolved (*Niddah* 61b). The reason that he says it is permissible to be buried in a forbidden shroud, even though there will be mitzvah observance after the resurrection, is that even though mitzvah will be performed in the future, they will not take the form of a commandment but rather will be undertaken because they are the will of God. Therefore it is permissible to bury a person in a forbidden shroud, since when he is resurrected there will be no "command" against wearing such a garment. Assumedly, when the dead arise they will miraculously not be wearing the forbidden clothes, since they are in opposition to God's will. Therefore, as the Rambam rules, "Jewish Law (as the will of God) is eternal," and as Rav Yosef holds, "mitzvahs (as Burdensome commandments) will be nullified in the future." See *Sefer HaSichos*, ibid, n. 45.

A fire engine arrived, and begged the scholar to leave the building; however he continued to pray that he would be saved—from above—and consequently ignored their pleas.

Then a police helicopter appeared, and demanded that the scholar go up to the roof, and they would rescue him from the furnace which now engulfed him. However, the scholar ignored these requests also, and continued to pray for redemption from the inferno.

It was not long before the scholar appeared before the Heavenly Tribunal. He complained bitterly that his faith had not been rewarded, and he had not been helped out of the fire.

"What do you mean 'you weren't helped'?" the scholar was told. "We sent you friends, a fire engine, and a helicopter to help, and you ignored them all."

EGO—EDGE GOD OUT

At the current time, when the world is in a state called "exile," a person feels his own identity and his own ego to the extent that "what God wants" is beyond his appreciation.[23] The "exile mentality" ensures a lack of awareness as to all that the "heavens" require of us,

---

23. Hence, the Rebbe recommends that the most straightforward way to bring about the coming of the Messiah is to study the explanations in the Torah relating to his coming, particularly in Mystical/Chassidic texts (see *Sefer HaSichos* 5751, vol. 2 [KPS, 1992], p. 501). The reason is that the Godly content of the Torah has the power to raise a person above their own concerns, and to appreciate those of God, particularly in matters of redemption, which are difficult to appreciate and internalize, due to the "exile mentality."

and so even the mitzvah which we have some understanding of appear somewhat burdensome. However, when the Messianic Redemption arrives, and the Jewish people are elevated to an infinitely higher level, the concept of mitzvahs as "burdensome commandments" will not be experienced: they will simply be appreciated for the "will of God" which they contain. Consequently, Rav Yosef is right, so that "mitzvahs [as commands] will be nullified in the future," but the Rambam is also correct, since "Jewish Law [as the will of God] is eternal."[24]

The way in which *tzedakah* is appreciated today is under the category of a mitzvah or a commandment, which means that it could be considered arduous by a person, that he is legally obliged to give away his money to the poor: nevertheless, since it is required by God, he determines to do so. The reason that he deems it burdensome is due to the fact that he experiences his own agenda and ego, and they directly interfere with the necessity to fulfil God's will. Even when he eventually decides to perform the mitzvah, there is often some feeling of pain and self-sacrifice.

However, when the Messiah comes, these obstacles will cease to exist, and the mitzvah of *tzedakah* will be performed as an invaluable and indispensable part of "Jewish Law"—not as a handicap imposed upon every human, but as a delightful activity which is appreciated as being the will of God, and the perfect means of connecting to Him.

---

24. See *Sefer HaSichos* 5752, vol. 1 (KPS, 1993), p. 31.

Index

About the Authors

Eli M. Shear is a barrister in London, England. His specialties include the law of charities, and he is a member of The Honourable Society of the Inner Temple. He has written a variety of articles for Jewish and legal publications, and is a well-known speaker on contemporary Jewish issues. Mr. Shear resides in London with his U.S.-born wife, Leah, and their daughter, Sara Yehudis.

Rabbi Chaim Miller recieved his rabbinical ordination at The Central Lubavitch Yeshiva in Brooklyn, New York. A respected author and lecturer, Rabbi Miller has published two halachic works: *A Practical Guide to the Korban Pesach* and *A Practical Guide to Bikurim*. He currently resides in Crown Heights, New York, with his wife, Chani.